The First 24 Hours of the American Revolution

An Hour by Hour Account of the Battles of Lexington, Concord, and the British Retreat on Battle Road

Jack Darrell Crowder

For Blair
my road trip companion and best friend since 1961

Copyright © 2018
Jack Darrell Crowder
All Rights Reserved

Printed for Clearfield Company by
Genealogical Publishing Company
Baltimore, Maryland
2018

ISBN 9780806358826

TABLE OF CONTENTS

Preface: ………………………………......……………..4

Prologue: ……………………...….……..…....………..5

Maps…………………………………….……………….7

Part I: The British March and the Alarm is Given………….11

Part II: Alarms Given to Other Towns in the Area……..........37

Part III: The Battle of Lexington……………………….55

Part IV: The Battle of Concord……………...………….67

Part V: Battle Road from Concord to Lexington……………..80

Part VI: Battle Road from Lexington to Boston……...……..87

Part VII: Back to Boston…………………………………97

Part VIII: Losses……………………………...….……..102

Part IX: Propaganda of Lexington and Concord …………..106

Conclusion…………………………………….....……..116

Index……………………………………………………118

Bibliography……………………………………...……..124

PREFACE

"Great results can be achieved with small forces." -----Sun Tzu, The Art of War

When I was a school boy I learned about the Battle of Lexington and Concord. I was taught that a bunch of farmers with rifles traded shots with British troops, a few people were killed, and it was the start of the Revolutionary War. After a few sentences the textbook moved on to George Washington cutting down a cherry tree and his famous battles. In other words I knew nothing of the Lexington and Concord story.

Fast forward fifty years and I was researching the Revolutionary War for several books I was writing. Many times I saw the statement, *"he answered the Lexington alarm"* or *"he died at Battle Road."* So, I thought that I needed to learn more about this famous battle, and who *"he"* was.

I read a couple of books on the topic, or scanned them in some cases and found them to be lacking clarity. They contained a wealth of information but it was hard to piece the Concord and Lexington battles together. I just wanted to know what happen that day and not all the background information I had to wade through.

That became the birth of this book. This is a concise story of the beginning and end of that eventful day, and telling hour by hour what each side was doing. I wanted the viewpoint of the common man and woman included in the story, so there are many eyewitness accounts. I wanted this book to be a personal account of how the average people felt, how they died, and how they suffered. I also felt it was necessary to find out how each side viewed the events of the day.

The Battles of Lexington, Concord, and Battle Road was the beginning of an eight year war against what most people thought were impossible odds. It was a story of courage and sacrifice of a small group of husbands, wives, sons, and daughters, who for the most part are forgotten to history.

Some of the information obtained on these men come from their own words in various books and documents. Their words and the documents are in the original wording and spelling, and they have not been changed. Much of the information is from sources written over a hundred years ago and out of print.

PROLOGUE

Since there was no standing army in the colonies, they formed independent local militias for their protection. During the French and Indian Wars of 1754-1763 the militia was called out to aid the British Army in responding to Indian attacks. The men were paid as long as they were called out, and several times a year they would train as a group. Training would increase to several times a week, if the chance for war increased. In Massachusetts all able men between 16 and 60 were expected to serve in the militia.

As problems with Great Britain began to rise, Massachusetts saw the need to have special units who were ready to turn out at a minute's notice when there was an emergency. The Provincial Congress passed a resolution on October 26, 1774 for the formation of minutemen. It stated that the militias in Massachusetts enlist companies to "hold themselves in readiness on the shortest notice from the said committee of safety, to march to the place of rendezvous…"

The minutemen were volunteers who trained more often and were usually paid an average of one shilling each time they trained. In most cases they served until the emergency was over, which usually was a term of several days. Many of the minutemen that served in the Battle of Lexington and Concord served for around five days, and because the threat continued many enlisted in the militia for eight months. Their officers, like in the militia, were selected by vote, and most of the time the leading citizens were named officers. Men that served in the French and Indians War were also given positions of command. Strangely enough Lexington did not have a minuteman company, but rather they had a militia.

Who were these minutemen? Most were farmers and shop keepers with practically no military experience. The majority of the minutemen were under the age of thirty-five, and some were even teenagers. Jeremiah Baker and Levi Smith, both 14 years old, answered the Lexington Alarm and marched on April 19, 1775. Both boys later joined the militia, and Levi fought at the Battle of Bunker Hill.

Some of them were "men of the cloth." Pastor Benjamin Balch marched with the minutemen from Danvers and participated at Battle Road. Seven of his friends from town were killed that day. Pastor Samuel Payson of Chelsea took up his musket and led the men in his congregation in attacking the British along Battle Road.

The women also did their part that day. In Pepperell, Massachusetts Prudence Wright's husband answered the Lexington alarm of the 19th, as did nearly all the men in town. Prudence organized the women in town to guard the vital road that passed through town. This road could be used to send messages from the British in Boston to the British north of town. The women dressed in men's clothing and gathered weapons to stop anyone from passing along the road. During the night they captured two of the enemy and turned them over to American forces.

African Americans answered the alarm on April 19th. Silas Burdoo, a former slave, fought at Lexington and later served for eleven months in the army. James Arcules, also free, fought at

Battle Road and later at Bunker Hill. Caesar Ferrit and his son John arrived at Lexington in time to fire at the British troops. Later, John Ferrit joined his father and brother and fought the British on Battle Road.

Tension began to increase between the colonists and the British and reached the boiling point in April of 1775. Men like Samuel Adams were doing everything they could to start a revolt. Militias were being organized, and arms and ammunition were being hidden away in anticipation of fighting between the patriots and British. Tempers began to flare between the patriots and the British sympathizers called Tories or Loyalists.

British General Gage commanded a force of nearly 3,500 men stationed in Boston. He recently discovered that the patriots had secretly taken arms and ammunition out of Boston and hid them in outlying towns. For weeks he had been sending officers in disguise to draw sketches of the roads, bridges, guard postings, and to get a feel of the mood of the people in the towns.

The Rev. William Emerson of Concord recorded in his diary that in February of 1775 there was enough military equipment stashed in Concord to supply 15,000 men. The supplies included tents, lead balls, rum, salt, cloth, and medicine. On April 8th Paul Revere was dispatched to Concord to warn the people that the British might be planning an expedition to Concord.

Fearing the supplies were a tempting target for General Gage, the patriots in Concord began to hide the supplies in the surrounding area and moved some of them to other towns. Weapons were buried in fields, and musket balls by the sack full were hidden in a nearby Concord swamp.

General Gage was under pressure from his King, George III, to put an end to the talk of rebellion. The King ordered Gage to capture the offensive Samuel Adams and John Handcock and ship them in chains to England to be tried for high treason.

General Gage received information from a spy within the Provincial Congress that delegates were being sent to the other colonies in New England to get them to join Massachusetts in raising an army in New England of 18,000 men. Gage decided that now was the time to act and rid himself of these meddlesome traitors. In a surprise move he sent a force of British regulars to Concord to capture the supplies and at the same time capture Adams and Hancock who were in the area. This would end talk of a rebellion and prove to the traitors that British rule was not to be taken lightly.

Events were about to unfold that would change the world. Once they were in motion there would be no going back. Both sides would refuse to compromise, and each would settle for nothing less that complete victory.

Maps

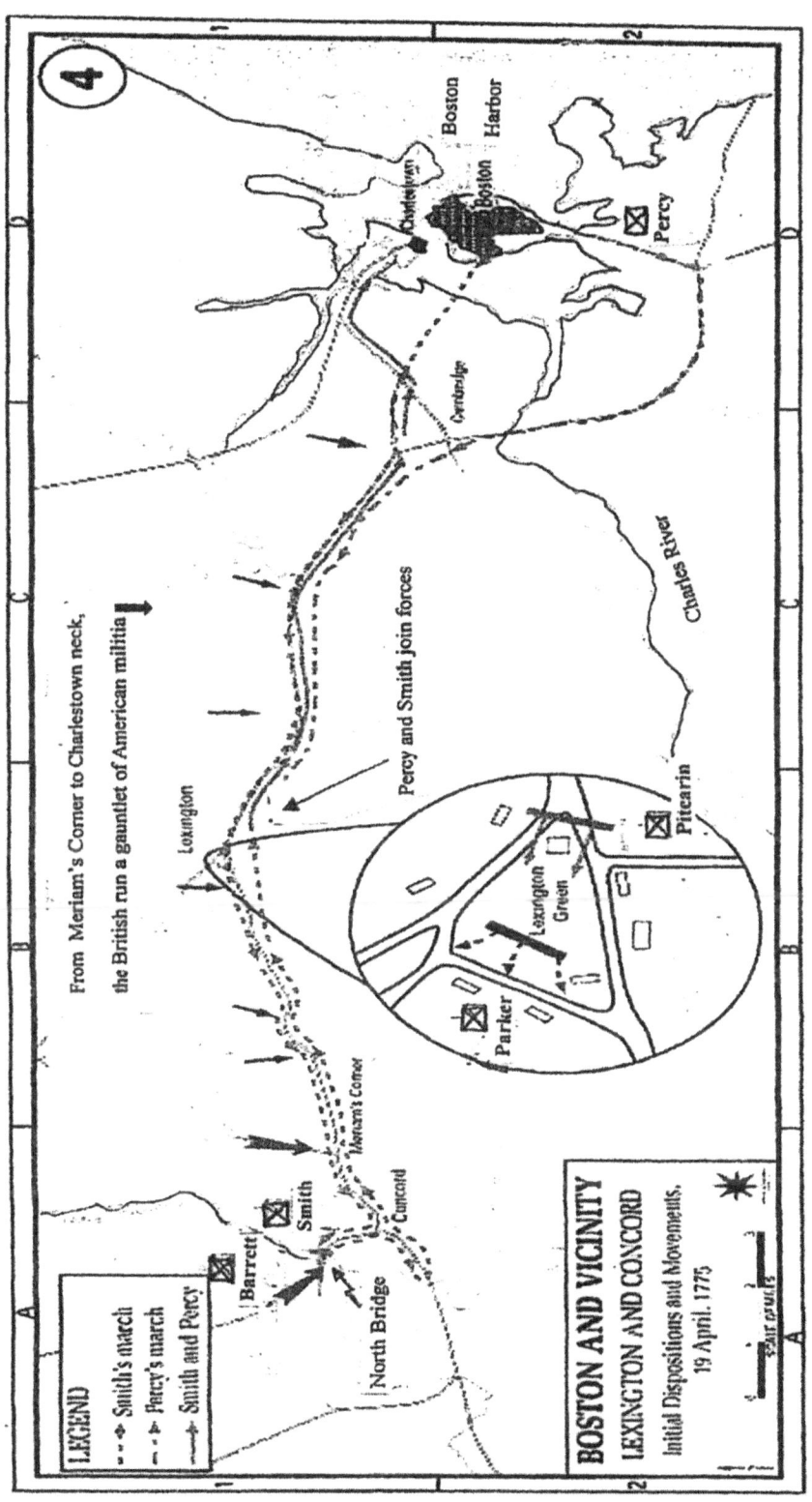

Map Courtesy of the USMA, Department of History

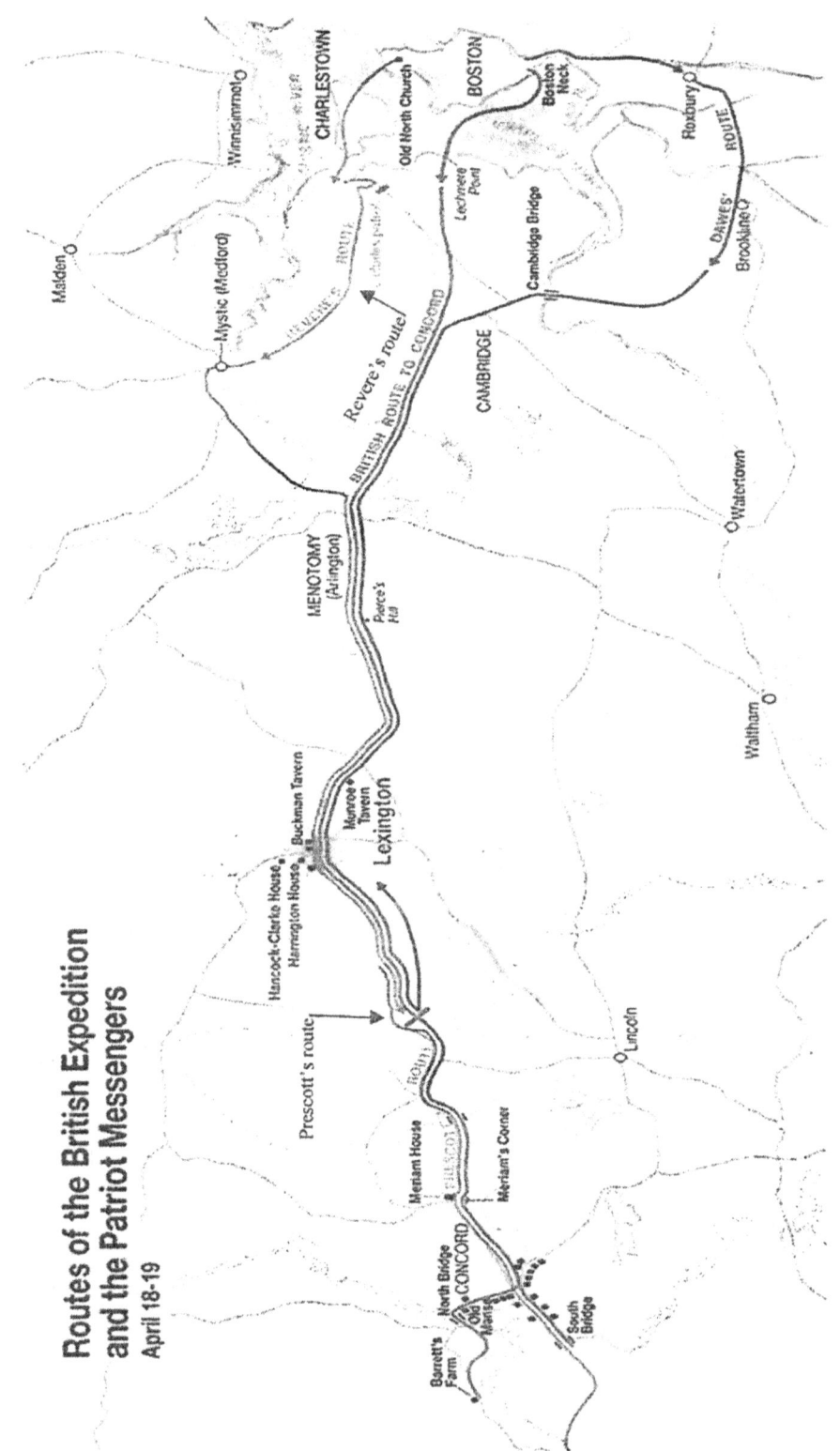

Map Courtesy of the National Park Service

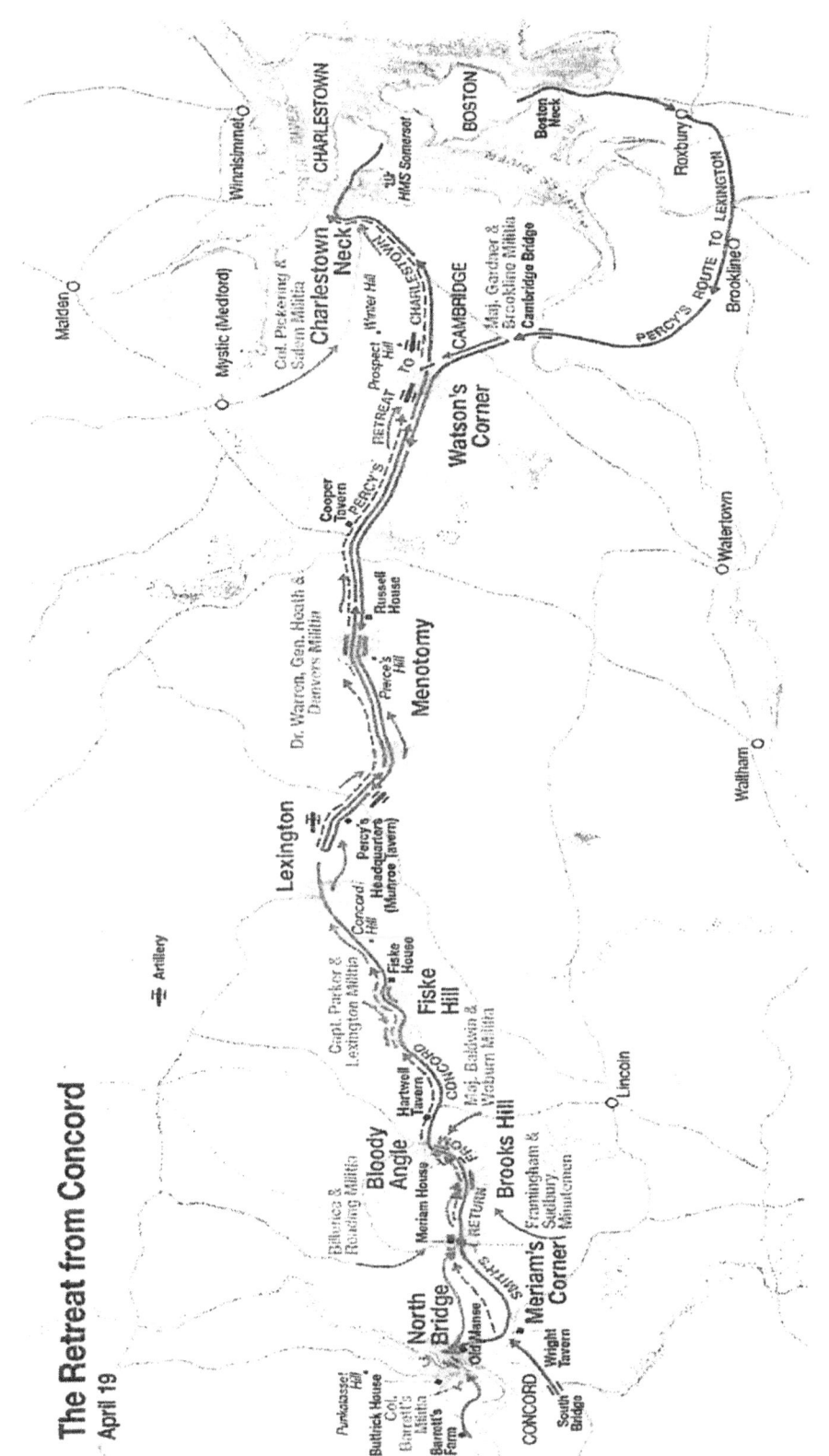

Map Courtesy of the National Park Service

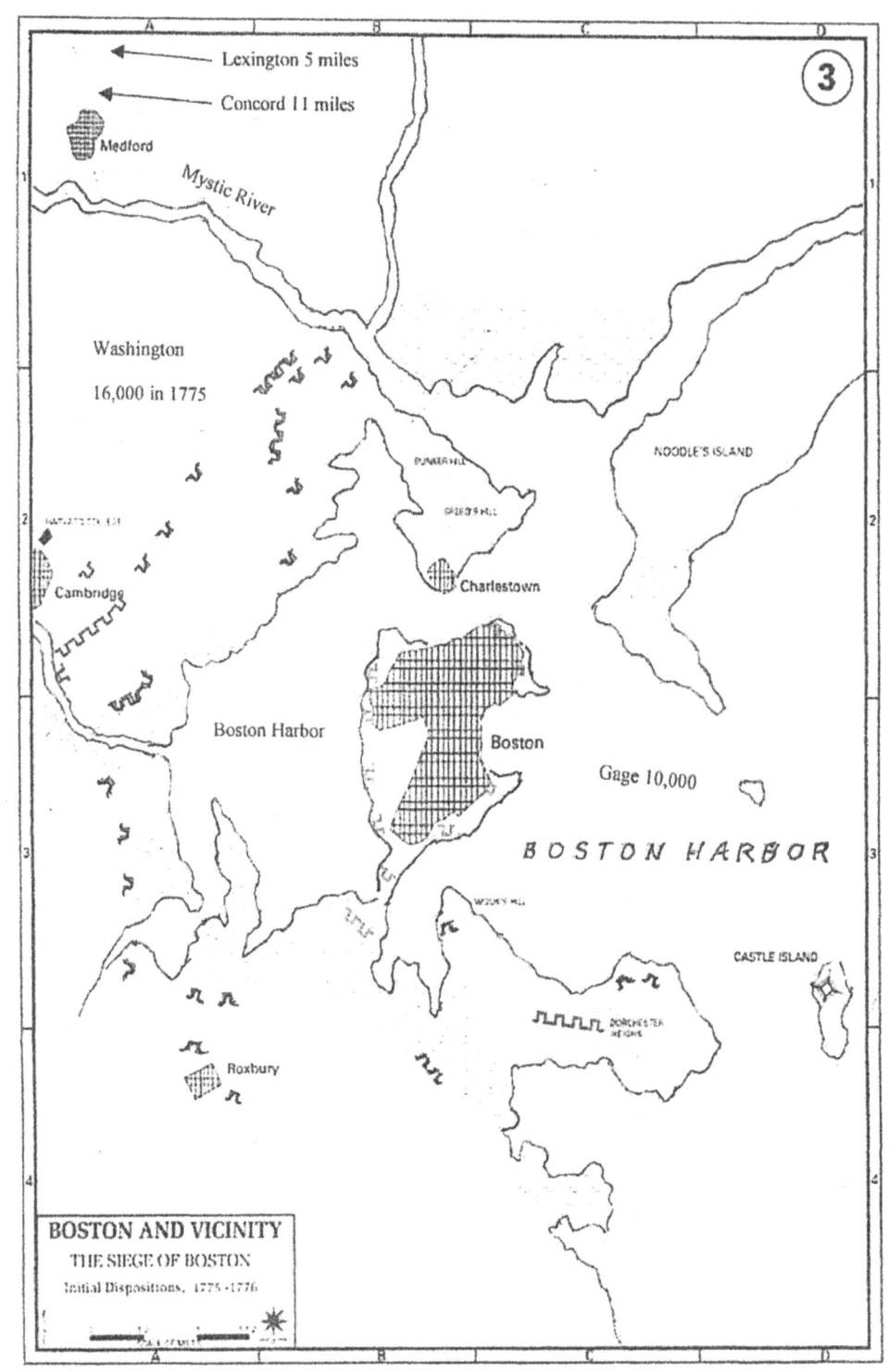

Map Courtesy of the USMA, Department of History

PART I

THE BRITISH MARCH AND THE ALARM IS GIVEN

"What a glorious morning is this!"

----Samuel Adams hours before the Battle at Lexington

Setting the Stage:

The morning of Tuesday April 18th, 1775 is unusually warm for this season of the year. A cold front passes through the area about noon bringing an end to showers and ushering in fair skies. British General Gage orders about twenty mounted troops under the command of Major Mitchell to ride into the surrounded countryside and intercept messengers who will be out on horseback. His troops will march on Concord that night, and the General does not want the towns around Boston warned in advance. Later in the morning Lieutenant Colonel Francis Smith of the 10th Infantry is summoned by Gage. He is told that he is to command an expedition, but he is not told where he is going. Colonel Smith is given sealed orders and told not to open them until he is on his way that night. Secrecy is of the upmost importance for the rest of the day.

General Thomas Gage. Engraving (bust). National Archives.

Rebel eyes are all over Boston, and they notice that transports and boats are being assembled and fitted for immediate service in the Charles River. Among the civilians this act creates suspicion that some military expedition is intended, but what, when, or where is anybody's guess. Joseph Warren, a thirty-four year old doctor and surgeon in Boston and an ardent patriot, learns in the afternoon about British troop movements. The doctor gathers the information from a gunsmith named Jasper, who hears it from a British sergeant.

John Ballard, a young man who runs the stables on Mild Street, overhears a British officer say "There would be Hell to pay tomorrow." Rumors are flying and anticipation fills the streets of Boston on this Tuesday.

Dr. Joseph Warren Portrait by John Singleton Copley, c. 1765.

6:30 p.m. April 18, 1775

The Americans: Solomon Brown, the eighteen year old son of a local deacon, returns home to Lexington from the market in Boston, and is passed by a group of British officers on the road. They ride away from Boston toward Lexington, which seems to Solomon to be most unusual. "Why are these officers riding away from Boston at near night fall?" Solomon asks himself. Solomon stays close to the riders for a while to see if he can learn their intentions. Several times he passes them and then allows them to repass him later. Solomon is convinced that the soldiers are not on a pleasure ride, so he gains the lead once again. When he is out of their sight he spurs his horse on to Lexington.

John Hancock and Samuel Adams attended the Massachusetts Provincial Congress in Concord and are hesitant of returning to Boston, so they stay at the home of the Reverend Jonas Clarke in Lexington. The house is the boyhood home of John Hancock and was built by his grandfather. It is two and a half stories with two rooms on each of the two floors.

John Hancock

Samuel Adams

The Hancock-Clarke House, a historical house and museum in Lexington, Massachusetts. CC BY-SA 3.0

The British: The officers that Solomon Brown encounters on the road to Lexington know that hostilities are at hand. During their ride along the road they detain travelers on the highway. The officers question the people and inquire as to where they have been and where they are going. They probably do not detain Solomon, because they believe the youth poses no risk.

The behavior of the officers goes beyond the behavior of military men in peacetime. They deliberately insult a number of the inhabitants along the way. When they reach the outskirts of Lexington, they stop at the house of Matthew Mead. They enter his home and help themselves to the family supper of brown bread and baked beans that are prepared. Mrs. Mead and her daughter are alone and can do nothing to stop the British from taking their meal. Mrs. Mead will have quite a story to tell her husband and two sons when they later return home.

Back in Boston the British troops are having their evening meal, and they are still unaware of the mission they are about to go on. General Gage is feeling confident that his rebel problems will soon be a thing of the past.

7:00 p.m. April 18, 1775

The Americans: Solomon Brown stops at William Munroe's tavern, a local meeting place for the people in the area, to tell Sergeant Munroe of the Lexington militia what he saw on the road. He reports that he saw nine British officers traveling leisurely on the road, and he discovers, "by the occasional blowing aside of their top coats, that they are armed." Fearing for the safety of Hancock and Adams, Sergeant Munroe gathers eight men from his company, and they stand watch at the Hancock-Clarke home.

William Munroe's tavern

The British: Despite the effort of General Gage to keep his mission a secret, word begins to reach Dr. Warren that the British might march upon Concord. [The historian Samuel A. Drake posts a letter in the Boston *Sunday Herald* on July 6, 1879 stating that the source of this intelligence was none other than Margaret Gage, the New Jersey born wife of General Gage. She is sympathetic to the Colonial's cause and had a friendship with Dr. Warren. There is no proof of this accusation, but the information must have come from someone close to the General and deep in his confidence.]

7:30 p.m. April 18, 1775

The British: The British officers encountered by Solomon Brown ride through Lexington without making any attempt to arrest Hancock and Adams at the Hancock-Clarke house. The group continues to ride on to Lincoln about four miles southwest of Lexington.

The Americans: As soon as the British officers pass through Lexington about 40 minutemen gather at the Buchman Tavern on Lexington Green. The tavern is the headquarters of the militia. As the men eat and drink, the topic of conservation is undoubtedly about the British patrol that just passed by. They discuss what should be done about these men.

Buckman Tavern. CC BY 2.0

8:00 p.m. April 18, 1775

The British: Around this time the British patrol of officers pass the farmhouse of Sergeant Samuel Hartwell of the Lincoln minutemen. As they ride a mile or so toward Concord, they wheel about and ride back toward Lexington.

9:00 p.m. April 18, 1775

The British: As the British patrol nears Lexington, they come to the house of Josiah Nelson. Josiah lives on his farm with his wife Elizabeth and a young slave by the name of Peter. Besides owning a 130 acre farm Josiah is also a part owner with his brother of a hop house where they brew beer for the local taverns.

Awakened by the patrol as they approach his house, Josiah rushes outside to see who it is. It is dark and Josiah is still not fully awake, so he could not see that the men are British officers. Since Josiah has the task of riding to Bedford to give the alarm in case the British army appears, he asks, "Have you heard anything about when the Regulars are coming out?" [Before the fighting began the Americans would refer to the British soldiers as Regulars or Redcoats because the Americans still considered themselves as British.]

One of the officers pulls out his sword and replies, "We will let you know when they are coming!" He then strikes Josiah on the crown of his head, and cuts a long gash. Thus is drawn the first blood in the Battle of Lexington and Concord.

Nelson is taken prisoner and left in the care of some Tories that are acting as guides for the officers. The officers soon ride out, and the Tories tell Josiah to go inside and have his wife tend to his wound. They tell him they will release him, and he is to stay inside his home. One of the Tories threatens to burn down his house if Josiah gives out any warning. He is reminded again to stay inside and show no lights in his home.

As the Tories ride off, Elizabeth dresses the head wound her husband received. When she finishes, Josiah goes to the barn, saddles his horse, and rides off to Bedford over four miles to the north to let them know there are British in the area.

Note: There were several versions of this story given over the years. There were different variations of time, who was present, and the role that Josiah played. This author believes the above account may be the most likely.

The Americans: The Lexington men gathering at Buchman Tavern see the British patrol pass by and take the road to Concord. They decide to send scouts out to trail the patrol to see what they are up to. Elijah Sanderson, Jonathan Loring, and Solomon Brown volunteer to trail them.

Back in Boston, the British: Lieutenant Colonel Smith has not opened his orders, so all he knows is that he must have his men on the beach to board boats by ten o'clock. The British soldiers are awakened in their barracks and told to prepare for a march.

General Thomas Gage sends for Lieutenant General Hugh Percy. Percy joined the British army as a teenager and quickly rose through the ranks. He will resign his command in 1777 over disagreements with General William Howe. Gage tells Percy that he will send troops to Concord to seize the stores (supplies), and asks him to keep it a secret.

Hugh Percy, 2nd Duke of Northumberland (1742-1817). PD-US

Percy leaves Gage and is walking back to his quarters, when he notices a group of people talking in a group. He wraps his cloak around himself to conceal his identity and listens to their conservation. He overhears one of the men say that the British are marching that night, and the object of the march is the stores in Concord.

Percy hurries back to General Gage to alert him that the secret is out. When Gage is told the news he sends out orders that no townspeople are to leave Boston that night.

Back in Boston, the Americans: Dr. Joseph Warren has heard the news that the British are going to March on Concord. He sends for Paul Revere and William Dawes, Jr. Paul Revere is a well-known express rider and had made a ride to Concord on April 8th to warn the residents that the British might march on their town to capture their military supplies.

William Dawes, "the forgotten man." PD-US

William Dawes is a patriot that has little love or fear of the British. On one occasion he succeeded in smuggling two cannons past British guards and out of Boston. Another time he and his wife were walking along Cornhill Street in Boston. It was after sundown, and William was walking ahead with a friend with his wife close behind. A British soldier standing near was attracted by the charms of Mrs. Dawes and swept her into his arms. She was a small woman, and thinking she was alone he attempted to carry her off. William turned on the soldier and gave the man a well-deserved beating.

Dr. Warren sends Dawes out of Boston to carry the alarm to towns on the way to Lexington. Dawes route will take him to the south through Cambridge, Roxbury, Brookline, Brighton, and then to Lexington. His route is four miles longer than the route of Paul Revere.

Revere leaves Dr. Warren and must make arrangements to send a signal to other additional riders across the Charles River. He tells the men to look to the steeple of Old North Church for the signal, to let them know when the British are leaving and by which route. One lit lantern means the British will take the longer route and march over the Boston Neck, a narrow strip of land. Two lit lanterns means the British will take the shorter route across the Charles River and into Cambridge.

9:30 p.m. April 18, 1775

Revere calls upon a childhood friend Captain John Pulling. He tells Pulling to go to the Old North Church and give the signal. Pulling meets Robert Newman at the church, and Newman, the church caretaker, unlocks the doors to the church. The two men enter and lock the doors behind them and climb one of the back staircases. They then go behind the pipe organ and through a small door that leads to the tower. In darkness they climb a series of stairs and ladders, and they go up eight stories.

Paul Revere then hurries to his home in North Square, puts on his boots and overcoat, and leaves for the wharf near the Charlestown ferry where his boat is moored. He knows that he must hurry, because the moon will rise soon. He meets two friends, Joshua Bently and Thomas Richardson, who row Revere across the river. Their oars are muffled by a petticoat, "yet warm from the body of a fair daughter of Liberty."

They leave just minutes before the sentinels receive orders to not allow any Americans to pass the lines. For the rest of the night all further crossings are forbidden to anyone.

9:45 p.m. April 18, 1775

Pulling and Newman having climbed the eight stories to the church steeple, they light the two lanterns, open the window, and hold both lanterns facing toward Charlestown for about one minute. Next, they extinguish the lanterns and hurry back to the first floor of the church.

The lanterns are seen by the patriots across the Charles River and also by British sentries. Pulling and Newman reach the first floor, climb through an open window by the main altar, and disappear into the dark streets of Boston. Pulling later disguises himself as a sailor, escapes from Boston in a fishing vessel, lands in Nantucket, and does not return to Boston until after the siege of Boston in the spring of 1776.

British soldiers arrive at the church and seek out the sexton of the church, and place him under arrest. The sexton denies any knowledge as to who displayed the lanterns in the steeple, and the soldiers release him.

Richard Deavens, a member of the Committee of Safety, is across the river and sees the signal from the church steeple. He immediately sends an express rider to Lexington to warn John Hancock and Samuel Adams that the Redcoats are coming out.

The boat carrying Paul Revere rows pass the anchored British man-of-war *Somerset* by using the shadows of the Boston skyline. They are now approaching the Charlestown shore.

10:00 p.m. April 18, 1775

The British: The 700 British infantry troops are assembled on the beach of the Charles River. They still do not know what their mission is and begin to stand around and grumble, because their commander Colonel Smith is late to arrive. Smith, a portly professional soldier, has no concept of time, and tardiness is something that he is accustomed too. He is selected for this command, because he is the senior officer.

The second in command is Major John Pitcairn, who is a very able officer of high character and he is well respected by friend and foe alike. He may have been assigned by General Gage, because he is ready to carry out his assignment with speed and insure that the troops do no plundering during the expedition.

Lieutenant Colonel Francis Smith {PD-1923}   Major John Pitcairn PD-1923}

The troops were selected from about two dozen various units, and the majority of the captains commanding them were volunteers who are attached to the units at the last minute. The unhappy troops do not know where they are going, are not familiar with their commanders, and they are missing a night's sleep.

These men are not fond of their duty in the colonies. They are far from home, among unfriendly people, even despised by many of them, which includes their own officers. They are paid less than a chimney sweep and not well respected even in England. There is a popular British warning at the time, "A messmate before a shipmate, a shipmate before a stranger, a stranger before a dog, and a dog before a soldier."

Military life is harsh, and most soldiers stay in the service for only as long as they can stand it. As a result, they are prone to getting drunk as often as they can. Major Pitcairn reported one time that he lost seven men "killed by drinking the cursed rum of the country." He once said that rum would, "kill more of us than Yankees will."

The British troops are also prone to desertion. General Gage once transferred a number of troops in New York by sea, rather than marching them overland for fear that he would lose half his army. The colonists capitalize on this by forming an underground railroad for defecting recoats. Nicholas Johnston was born in Scotland and came to this country as a thirteen year old British solider. He deserts in 1778 at the age of fourteen and floats down the Hudson River in winter to join the American Army.

Shortly after ten o'clock, Lieutenant Colonel Francis Smith arrives, and the British troops begin to disembark for Lechmere Point. They use naval barges, and the troops are packed in so tight that they cannot sit down. It requires several trips to carry all the troops across the river. Because of the late arrival of Smith and his lack of having the men move as quickly as possible they do not reach the shore a few hundred yards away and aren't ready to march until almost two a.m.

The Americans: William Dawes gives the alarm in Cambridge and then reaches Roxbury. Outside of Lexington the three American volunteer scouts are following the British officers, who soon turn south toward Lincoln. After about three miles the Americans ride around a sharp bend in the road and they come face to face with the British officers who are facing them and blocking the road.

The following article is from the *Eastern Argus* April 28, 1825 describing the event,

> I, ELIJAH SANDERSON, of Salem, in the country of Essex, cabinet-maker, aged seventy-three years, on oath depose as follows:

> "In this spring of 1775, I resided in Lexington, and had resided there then more than a year. In the spring of that year, the officers of the British regular troops in Boston were frequently making excursions, in small parties into the country, and often, in the early part of the day, In pleasant weather, passed through Lexington, and usually were seen returning before evening. I lived then on the main road, about three quarters of a mile east of the meeting house."

> "On the evening of the 18th of April, 1775, we saw a party of officers pass up from Boston, all dressed in blue wrappers. The unusually late hour of their passing excited the attention of the citizens. I took my gun and cartridge box and thinking something must be going on more than common, walked up to John Buckman's tavern near the meeting house. After some conversation among the citizens assembled there, an old gentleman advised, that someone should follow those officers and endeavor to ascertain their object. I then observed, that if anyone would let me have a horse, I would go in pursuit. Thaddeus Harrington told me I might take his, which was there. I took his, and Solomon Brown proposed to accompany me on his own horse. Jonathan Loring also went with us. We started, probably about nine o'clock; and we agreed, if we could find the officers, we would return and give information, as the fears were, that the object was, to come back in the night, and seize Hancock and Adams, and carry them into Boston. It had been rumored, that the British officers had threatened, that Hancock and Adams should not stay at Lexington. They had been boarding some time at Parson Clarke's."

> "We set out in pursuit. Just before we got to Brook's in Lincoln, while riding along, we were stopped by nine British officers, who were paraded across the road. They were all

mounted. One rode up and seized my bridle, and another my arm, and one put his pistol to my breast, and told me, if I resisted, I was a dead main. I asked what he wanted. He replied he wanted to detain me a little while. He ordered me to get off my horse. Several of them dismounted and threw down the wall, and led us into the field. They examined and questioned us where we were going &c. Two of them staid in the road, and the other seven with us relieving each other from time to time. They detained us in that vicinity till a quarter past two o'clock at night. An officer, who took out his watch, informed me what the time was. It was a bright moon light after the rising of the moon, and a pleasant evening. During our detention, they put many questions to us, which I evaded. They kept us separately, and treated us very civilly. They particularly inquired where Hancock and Adams were; also about the population. One said. 'You've been numbering the inhabitants, have not ye?' I told him how many it was reported there were. One of them spoke up and said. 'There were not so many, men, women and children.' They asked as many questions as a Yankee could."

11:00 p.m. April 18, 1775

The Americans: Paul Revere reaches the shore of Charlestown still unnoticed. He walks into the town and meets with Colonel Conant, Richard Deavens, and a few other men. Deavens has a strong and swift horse named Brown Beauty prepared for Revere. While the horse is being saddled, he tells Revere that he came down the road from Lexington after sundown and met ten British officers, all mounted and well-armed, going up the road. Deavens and Revere walk into Mr. Larkin's barn, and Revere mounts Brown Beauty. Deavens tells Revere to give this intelligence at Menotomy and Lexington. Revere rides off knowing that ahead of him are roadblocks manned by the British, with orders to arrest anyone who attempts to raise an alarm. The distance to Lexington is about eleven miles and on Brown Beauty he should be there within the hour.

Shortly after leaving and beyond the Charlestown Neck, Revere is confronted by two British horsemen that are in the shadows under a tree at a crosswords. He later wrote, "I was near enough to see their holsters and cockades."

Revere turns his horse abruptly, gallops back toward the Neck, and takes the road to Medford. One of the British horsemen takes off after Revere and races across a field hoping to cut him off. Because of the recent rains the British soldier's horse gets mired in the soft ground around a pond. This gives Revere enough time to make his escape.

He then goes on a route around Cambridge rather than through it. This road will take Revere through Medford and will make his ride a little longer.

Paul Revere's ride, Illustration. National Archives

11:30 a.m. April 18, 1775

The Americans: Paul Revere reaches Medford and later wrote, "In Medford, I awaked the captain of the minutemen; and after that, I alarmed almost every house, till I got to Lexington."

Paul Revere and William Dawes are on the roads sounding the alarm. Each town they go to are sending out their own riders sounding the alarm. Richard Deavens also sends a rider to Lexington to warn Hancock and Adams. Once the signal from the Old North Church is given, many riders from the other side of the river leave to sound the alarm. During the evening riders are going all over the place sounding alarms, capturing or chasing each other, and maybe passing by each other.

The British: The British are still transporting their troops across the Charles River. Because the boats are heavily loaded they cannot reach the shore, so the troops must get out of the boat and wade through waist deep marsh water to reach the shore. When they reach the shore they begin to assemble in the road and wait for all the troops to be ferried across. The troops are tired, cold, and wet and will have to wait around in the dark until nearly two a.m.

12:00 a.m. Wednesday April 19, 1775

The Americans: Paul Revere arrives at the Hancock-Clarke House in Lexington just after midnight. He has been on the road a little more than an hour. Inside the house sleeping is John Hancock, John Adams, and family members. Sergeant Munroe and his men are guarding the outside of the house.

Revere demands to be let into the home, but Munroe who does not know Revere says, "The family has just retired and had requested that they might not be disturbed by any noise about the house." This angers Revere and he shouts back, "Noise? You'll have noise enough before long. The regulars are coming out."

Parson Clarke is awakened by the shouting outside his open window and he looks down below on the men talking and asks who is there. Revere hollers up to the parson that he wants to see John Hancock. Now, Hancock, is also awake, looks out the window, and recognizes Revere as a friend. He yells down, "Come in Revere, we are not afraid of you."

Sergeant Munroe steps aside and Revere enters the house. As Hancock and Adams gather around him. Revere tells them of the news from Boston and how he was almost captured. He then expresses concern for his fellow rider Dawes. Revere hands Hancock a note from Dr. Warren that that states that the British are sending about 1,200 to 1,500 troops, and they are going to destroy the stores in Concord.

The news of the British marching toward Concord must have been very pleasing to Samuel Adams. Just one shot from a British musket and one dead patriot will give him the revolution he has been working for.

Also, Hancock is pleased with the news. He expects that the Second Congress will finally name him the commander-in-chief. He can now wear the gorgeous uniform he had custom made for himself, and he can lead the troops into battle against the British. This war with England will also free him from the hundreds of indictments for smuggling that are pressing in the courts. [He will later become very disappointed when Congress gives his coveted military position to George Washington.]

12:30 a.m. Wednesday April 19, 1775

The Americans: After traveling over sixteen miles William Dawes arrives at the Hancock-Clarke House. Both Revere and Dawes are elated to see each other safe. They sit down to take some quick refreshments before they leave for Concord. This will also give their mounts a chance to rest since there is now a shortage of horses in Lexington due to riders being sent out from the town.

The bell in the belfry that stands on Lexington Green near the meetinghouse rings out the alarm, and the Lexington militia under Captain John Parker begin to assemble. John Parker who lives a mile away on his farm is one of the most trusted men in town. [At forty-six he is in the late stages of tuberculosis and will die in September.] He is naturally thin and now he has become even thinner due to his disease. Because of the rumors of the British marching he has slept poorly during the night.

Parker sends his fourteen year old son John Jr. to stand near the road to be ready for any messages that need to be sent out. Parker's mother takes some of the family treasures and hides them outside in a hollow apple trunk.

Captain Parker sends a messenger to Buckman's tavern to request that some of the men there sound the alarm to the other militiamen that live further outside of town. Once the men are gathered on Lexington Green the roll is called, and Captain Parker instructs the men to load with powder and ball. One of the messengers Parker had sent toward Boston returns and reports that there are no British soldiers in sight. Some of the men begin to think that the alarm is false and no British will be coming. Parker continues to send messengers toward Boston through the night. He does not want his men taken by surprise.

Revere and Dawes finally mount their horses and ride out toward the west to Concord, which is nearly seven miles away. They ride out at a slower pace because their horses are still tired and they know they have ample time. On the way they are overtaken by twenty-three year old Doctor Samuel Prescott a native of Concord.

[According to tradition Dr. Prescott had been in Lexington visiting his sweetheart Lydia Mulliken.] The three men strike up a conversation and Prescott is told of the nine or ten British officers that had been seen on the road earlier in the night. When Revere is certain that Prescott is a "high Son of Liberty" he asks the young doctor to join them. Since Prescott is a country doctor he is familiar with the roads in the area and he will be of great help. Also, because the doctor knew the people in the area he could vouch for the genuineness of the alarm from Revere and Dawes.

1:00 a.m. Wednesday April 19, 1775

When the three riders are about halfway to Concord, Dawes and Prescott stop at a farmhouse to arouse the occupants, but Revere rides ahead. The road takes two sharp bends, and as Revere comes around the final bend he stops. Just ahead of him are two British officers under a tree at the side of the road. The night is clear, so he has no doubt that the men are British soldiers. Hoping to scare the men off, Revere calls loudly to Dawes and Prescott who are about a hundred yards behind him, "Here are two, we will have them." As Dawes and Prescott ride up, two more British officers appear coming from a pasture on the right where they had been standing in the shadow of a tree.

The British officers call out, "Damn you, stop, if you go an inch farther, you are a dead man." The officers corralled the three Americans and escort them into a pasture. Prescott turns to Revere and says, "Put on." Prescott immediately turns his horse to the left and jumps the pasture stone wall. He rides into a ravine, and because he knows the location well, he follows the road through the thicket until it comes out on the Concord road again a half mile beyond. Prescott will be the only one of the three to reach Concord that night to give the alarm. [In the poem *The Midnight Ride of Paul Revere* Longfellow will incorrectly give Revere the credit for reaching Concord.]

Paul Revere turns his horse to the right and heads toward a dense woods. He hopes that he can reach the woods, dismount, and seek safety among the thick trees. Six more officers suddenly appear and grab his bridle and order him to dismount.

Dawes turns his mount back toward Lexington with two of the officers in pursuit. Dawes races his horse up to a farmhouse. He falls from his horse and quickly jumps up and notices that the farmhouse is abandoned. Hoping to fool the soldiers he yells out to the imaginary occupants in the farmhouse, "Hallo, my boys. I've got two if 'em."

The ruse is successful, and the two officers fearing their own capture retreat. Dawes's horse has run off, so he must now walk back to Lexington. While walking back he notices that he lost his watch during the fall. Several days later he will return and find it.

Solomon Brown and his two companions had passed along this very place about ten o'clock and were detained and held as prisoners. Now Paul Revere is added to the group. A one handed peddler, by the name of Allen, is also held prisoner after being captured for some reason. Later Allen is released and he goes on his way.

The officer in charge, Major Mitchell, begins to question Revere. He asks where he came from, what time did he leave, and he asks his name. The officer tells Revere that he and his men were out looking for British deserters. Revere tells him that he knows better, and he is aware of what they were after. Revere says to the officer, "I have alarmed the county all the way up, and their boats were catch'd aground, and I should have 500 men there soon; one of them said they had 1,500 coming."

This appears to disturb the British. Major Mitchell puts a pistol to the head of Revere and tells him that he is going to ask some questions, and if Revere lies he will blow his brains out. The officer then asks Revere the same questions as before, and Revere gives the same answers. Revere is told to mount his horse, and the reins of the horse are given to a British Sergeant. The sergeant is ordered to blow the prisoner's brains out if he attempts to escape, or if any insults are offered to his captors on the way.

1:30 a.m. Wednesday April 19, 1775

Paul Revere and his captors get back on the road to Lexington, where they are joined by the other four captives and the rest of the British soldiers. An officer tells Revere, "We are now going toward your friends, and if you try to run, we will blow your brains out." It is nearly two o'clock, and when they approach within a half mile of Lexington they hear gunfire. This alarms Major Mitchel, because he believes that there might be rebel troops ahead. The gunfire in Lexington is the signal given for the militia to form.

The British cut the saddles and bridles from the horses of all the prisoners except for Revere. They drive the horses away and set the men free to leave on foot. As the prisoners walk away Mitchell asks Revere how far it is to Cambridge, and if other roads go there. Revere is then told to dismount. The British take Revere's horse and they ride off down the road toward Lexington, as Revere makes his way on foot across the old cemetery and the adjacent pasture near Lexington Common. From there he walks to the Hancock-Clarke House.

The British officers take a road that will by-pass Lexington. They are certain that Concord is alerted, and the American army might be in Lexington. Believing that their mission is over they ride back toward Boston.

Dr. Prescott emerges from a thicket behind the house of Sergeant Samuel Hartwell of the Lincoln minutemen. He wakes the family and requests that the news be carried to Captain William Smith of the Lincoln minutemen. Sulkey, a slave girl, is in terror of the British and refuses to leave the house. So, Mary Hartwell, the sergeant's wife, places her five month old infant in Sulkey's arms and rushes down the road to Captain Smith's house. Smith mounts a horse and hastens to Lincoln Center two miles to the south, where the two Lincoln companies assemble and start off for Concord. [They will be the first companies to reach Concord from any of the neighboring towns.]

The following article is from the April 28, 1825 *Eastern Argus* written by Elijah Sanderson, who was one of the three volunteer scouts captured by the British. He describes the capture of Paul Revere.

I, ELIJAH SANDERSON, of Salem, in the country of Essex, cabinet-maker, aged seventy-three years, on oath depose as follows:

"While we were under detention they look two other prisoners, one Allen, a one-handed peddler, and Col. Paul Revere; also they attempted to stop a man on horseback, who, we immediately after understood, was Dr. Prescott's son. He was well mounted, and, after turning from the road into the field toward us, he put spurs to his horse and escaped. Several of the officers pursued him, but could not overtake him."

"After they had taken Revere, they brought him within half a rod of me, and I heard him speak up with energy to them, 'Gentleman; you've missed of your aim!' Revere replied, 'I came out of Boston an hour after your troops had come out of Boston, and landed as Lechmere's Point, and if I had not known people had been sent out to give information to the country, and time enough to get fifty miles, I would have ventured one about from you, before I would have, suffered you to have stopped me.' Upon this they went little aside and conversed together. They then ordered me to untie my horse, (which was tied to a little birch) and mount. They kept us in the middle of the road, and rode on each side of us. We went toward Lexington."

"They took all of us, (Revere, Loring, and Brown and myself). My horse not being swift, and they riding at considerable speed, one of the officers pressed my horse forward, by striking him with his hanger. When we had arrived within fifty or one hundred rod of the meeting house, Loring (as he afterwards informed me) told them, 'The bell's a ringing, the towns alarmed, and you're all dead men.' They then stopped—conferred together. One then dismounted, and ordered me to dismount, and said to me, 'I must do you an injury.' I asked, what he was going to do with me now. He made no reply, but with his hanger cut my bridle and girth, and then mounted, and they rode in a good smart trot on toward Boston. We then turned off to pass through the swamp, through the mud and water, intending to arrive at the meeting house before they could pass, to give information to our people. Just before they got to the meeting house, they had bolted, which led us to hope, we should get there first; but they soon started off again at full speed, and we saw no more of them."

2:00 a.m. Wednesday April 19, 1775

The Americans: The militia in Lexington is milling around the common area waiting for news of the British advance. The scouts report no British are in sight, so Captain Parker dismisses his men and gives orders to respond again at the beating of the drum. Those who do not live near enough to go home walk over to Buchman Tavern. There the men begin to talk, eat, and definitely drink to take the chill out of the night air. Messengers are continuing to be sent out.

Sometime near three in the morning Dr. Prescott arrives in Concord and gives the alarm. One of the townsmen begins to ring the Town House bell. Grabbing his gun Reverend William Emerson, grandfather of Ralph Waldo Emerson, is the first to answer the alarm. Three companies of minutemen soon gather at Wright's Tavern in the town square. They begin the task of removing and concealing the military stores that were not sent away the day before.

Meliscent Barrett, the fifteen year old granddaughter of the Colonel of the Concord militia, has gathered some of the young women of Concord. Meliscent had learned from a British officer how to roll powder cartridges. She is now supervising her friends in preparing cartridges which will be used against the British at the North Bridge.

The British: The British finish their crossing of the Charles River around one-thirty, but they have to wait for their provisions to arrive. It is now two a.m. and has taken them four hours to travel several hundred yards. During the wait the soldiers are given extra ammunition, salt pork, and hard biscuits. There is no need to carry knapsacks, since they believe they will be back that night. They begin their march sleepy, tired, and cold in wet soggy uniforms.

British Lieutenant John Barker later writes, "At two o'clock we began our March by wading through a very long ford up to our Middles and after three or four miles we took three or four people who were going off to give intelligence."

The British are not aware that if they had saved two hours or even one hour, they would have passed through Lexington before daylight, and they could have started back to Boston earlier. Many events of the day that are about to happen might have been very different.

While the British troops are crossing the Charles River, Lt. Colonel Smith reads his orders from General Gage,

> "Having received intelligence, that a quantity of Ammunition, Provisions, Artillery, Tents and small Arms, have been collected at Concord, for the Avowed Purpose of raising and

supporting a Rebellion against His Majesty, you will March with a Corps of Grenadiers and Light Infantry, put under your Command, with the utmost expedition and Secrecy to Concord, where you will seize and destroy all Artillery, Ammunition, Provisions, Tents, Small Arms, and all Military Stores whatever. But you will take care that the Soldiers do not plunder the Inhabitants, or hurt private property."

"You have a Draught of Concord, on which is marked the Houses, Barns, &c, which contain the above military Stores. You will order a Trunion to be knocked off each Gun, but if it's found impracticable on any, they must be spiked, and the Carriages destroyed. The Powder and flower must be shook out of the Barrels into the River, the Tents burnt, Pork or Beef destroyed in the best way you can devise. And the Men may put Balls of lead in their pockets, throwing them by degrees into Ponds, Ditches &c., but no Quantity together, so that they may be recovered afterwards. If you meet any Brass Artillery, you will order their muzzles to be beat in so as to render them useless."

"You will observe by the Draught that it will be necessary to secure the two Bridges as soon as possible, you will therefore Order a party of the best Marchers, to go on with expedition for the purpose."

"A small party of Horseback is ordered out to stop all advice of your March getting to Concord before you, and a small number of Artillery go out in Chaises to wait for you on the road, with Sledge Hammers, Spikes, &c."

"You will open your business and return with the Troops, as soon as possible, with I must leave to your own Judgment and Discretion."

The orders state very clearly what is to be done, but the problem is Colonel Smith is not given a definite timeline. Smith is not noted for being punctual, so to order him to "open your business and return with the Troops, as soon as possible" gives the Colonel much latitude in his assignment. The troops begin their long anticipated march through the west end of Charlestown, and they take the road to Menotomy. Colonel Smith sends out two advanced scouts toward Lexington.

As they march through Cambridge the British soldiers pass by Samuel Tufts' house. He is making bullets with his Negro servant in a hut at the back of the house and does not hear them pass. Widow Elizabeth Rand, who lives nearby, hears them and runs in her night clothes to tell Tufts. Mr. Tufts instantly saddles his horse and gallops to warn others.

2:30 a.m. Wednesday April 19, 1775

The Americans: After leaving the British Paul Revere finally emerges from the field and arrives at the Hancock-Clarke House. This time the house is lit up with lights from every window. He is amazed to find that Hancock and Adams have not fled but are still inside the house.

Hancock, Adams, and Rev. Clarke are at a table talking, and nearby is Hancock's Aunt Lydia and his fiancée Dorothy Quincy. Hancock does not want to flee the approaching British troops. [According to his fiancée, Hancock had spent most of the night cleaning his pistol.] Adams finally convinces Hancock to flee by telling him, "this is not our business, we belong to the cabinet." Hancock gets the last word in, "If I had my musket, I would never turn my back on these troops." [Are Hancock's words that of a brave man, a foolish man, or a man trying to impress his fiancée?]

After Paul Revere tells the group of his recent adventures, they all agree that Hancock and Adams need to leave at once. Samuel Adams is not fond of riding a horse, so it is decided that they will leave by carriage. Sergeant Munroe leads the carriage that contains Hancock, and Adams, and Hancock's secretary John Lowell. Paul Revere travels with them, and Rev. Clarke's son Jonas drives the carriage. The ladies stay behind because it is considered safer and they can follow later.

As they prepare to leave, Adams exclaims, "What a glorious morning this is!" The others stare at Adams with a puzzled look. Adams sees that they do not understand his meaning, so he adds, "I mean for America!"

3:00 a.m. Wednesday April 19, 1775

The Americans: The small group flee about two miles north of Lexington, where Hancock and Adams are taken to a clump of woods. Here they hide and are still close to early intelligence. The men soon decide that it is better if they go to the house of Rev. Marrett in Burlington. When they reach Burlington, Munroe takes the carriage and heads back to Lexington. Hancock remembers his trunk is at Buchman Tavern, and it contains documents that will incriminate many of the patriot leaders in Massachusetts, if it should fall into British hands. Lowell and Revere agree to return to Lexington to retrieve the valuable chest.

The British: An advanced group of British troops are entering Menotomy, and now they are a little over 4 ½ miles from Lexington. As the 700 troops pass by the Newell Tavern at about three in the morning, they think they are still marching somewhat in secret but they are being watched. Old Samuel Whittemore who lives with his son and grandchildren is awakened by the stir in the street. When he looks out of his window he sees the bayonets shinning in the moonlight. Samuel's son Amos gets up later in the morning and repairs several old guns that were used in the French and Indian War. Samuel will be waiting for the British later in the day when they returned.

The day before three members of the Committee of Safety had a meeting in Cambridge and were spending the night at the Black Horse Tavern in Menotomy. They are Vice-President Elbridge Gerry and Colonels Lee and Orne. They get up and watch as the soldiers pass by. Gerry is about to open the door when the landlord cries out, "For God's sake don't open that door." He leads the three men to the back door, and they escape into the cornfield in their night clothes just before a British officer post guards about the doors. The tavern is searched and they find a gold watch under the pillow left by one of the men.

Solomon Bowman, a Lieutenant of the minutemen, comes to the door of his house and opens it. A British soldier, that broke ranks, asks him for a drink of water. Solomon refuses the man and wants to know what they are doing out so late. After the British pass Solomon leaves to warn his company. By morning the minutemen were ready to march.

Following his orders from General Gage, Lieutenant Colonel Smith sends Major Pitcairn and about 200 men ahead to seize the two bridges over the Concord River. Pitcairn knows that the colonists are gathering in front of him. He does not know where or how many there are. His orders are very clear, "do not fire unless fired upon." The British do not want to start a fight. He gallops up and down the column repeating this order to his men. Pitcairn sends an advance guard ahead of his men.

Further up the road the soldiers see a house with a light showing through the shutters. A soldier is sent to inquire why there is light in the house in the middle of the night. Inside, Captain Benjamin Locke's parents, Samuel and his wife Mehitable, are busy melting their pewter plates into bullets. When the soldier knocks at the door Samuel throws himself on the bed, and his wife empties the pan of melted pewter upon the fireplace ashes. She goes to the door and explains to the soldier that she is making herb tea for her sick husband. Mehitable would later tell the story to people and add, "It was a kind of herb tea the British had reason to dread after that day."

Two advanced scouts, Lieutenant Sutherland and Lieutenant Adair, are sent ahead by Lieutenant Colonel Smith, and they capture two of the American scouts sent from Lexington by Captain Parker.

3:30 a.m. Wednesday April 19, 1775

The British: Lieutenant Sutherland and Lieutenant Adair, the British advanced scouts, meet Major Mitchell and the officers who had earlier captured Paul Revere. Mitchell spins a tale of the whole country alive with militia, and that he and his men had to ride hard to save their lives. While the British officers are talking, they capture two more American riders from Lexington. The British decide that they need to return to the main force behind them.

On the ride back the soldiers see groups of militiamen going toward Lexington. They are able to capture one of them, thirty-two year old Benjamin Wellington. The British officer that captures him asks, "What are you going to do with that firelock? Where are you going now?"

"I'm going home," Benjamin replies. When Benjamin later told the story he said, "I thought within myself, but not until I have been upon the Common."

The British officer takes the firelock from the American, soon releases him and tells him to go home. Wellington leaves the main road, wades through some swamps, and reaches the Lexington Common. There he borrows a gun and joins the company under Captain Parker.

Lieutenant Colonel Smith knows that people in the countryside are aware that the British are marching toward Concord. He hears the sound of bells and gunfire in the distance. He sends a messenger back to General Gage in Boston to alert the General that things are not going well. They are three hours behind schedule, and they will enter Concord in broad daylight. He requests that the General send reinforcements at once to aid him. Captain Smith will later learn that this was the smartest thing he did all day, for without the request it is unlikely that he or his men would have made it back to Boston alive.

The Americans: In Lexington Captain Parker is concerned, because none of the scouts he has sent out have returned. All of Parker's militiamen have gone home except for a couple dozen of his men at Buchman's Tavern. Revere and Lowell are nearing Lexington to retrieve the trunk belonging to Hancock.

4:00 a.m. Wednesday April 19, 1775

The British: The group of British scouts encounter Major Pitcairn and inform the major that there are perhaps thousands of militiamen ahead of them. Major Pitcairn cannot turn back to the main force of British troops, because he has his orders. The Major knows a good British soldier follows orders regardless of the odds against him. He orders his men to load and prime their muskets. Now ready for battle they march on toward Lexington.

Back in Boston General Gage fears that Colonel Smith will need some reinforcements, so he writes out orders for the 1st Brigade to have their companies form at once. Gage believes that the mission is still a well-kept secret, so he sends only one copy of the orders to the adjutant in the 1st Brigade. The orders are passed to the adjutant's servant, who places them on a table where they sit unopened.

4:15 a.m. Wednesday April 19, 1775

The Americans: The fourth scout sent out by Captain Parker is Thaddeus Bowman. At four-fifteen that morning he comes in a full gallop into Lexington. He found the British, and he is late getting back because he was trapped behind them. He tells Captain Parker they are already past "the rocks". This landmark indicates that the British are only a half an hour away.

Parker summons his men to muster, and he orders nineteen year old William Diamond to beat "to arms" to alert the men. William learned to play on the town's new drum weeks earlier. In addition the town bell begins to ring and alarm guns begin to fire. The British are coming through Lexington, and Captain Parker has no intention of stopping them. However, if forced to, he will protect the town, women, and children.

Parker has Sergeant Munroe march the men onto the common. The only music comes from William Diamond's drum and the flute from Jonathan Harrington. The men form two lines on the open green away from the road. Parker wants to show the determination of the militia, but he does not want to block the road or provoke a fight. He gives his orders to his men to let the British pass.

Elijah Sanderson many years later tells his story to *The Independent Chronicle and Boston Patriot*,

"I went into the tavern. The citizens were coming and going; some went down to find whether the British were coming; and some came back, and said there was no truth in it. I went to the tavern, and after awhile, went to sleep in my chair by the fire. In a short time after, the drums beat, and I ran out to the Common, the militia were parading. The Captain ordered them to fall in. I then fell in. The British troops were then coming on in full sight."

Around this time Revere and Lowell arrive at the tavern, and they go inside to get Hancock's trunk. They procure the trunk and as they leave, and have to pass through the militia on the green. Having nothing to defend themselves with Lowell and Revere leave the area and hide in the woods.

Confusion among the men on the green begins to appear. Some have no ammunition, so they leave to go to a nearby meetinghouse for some. Some men came without weapons, and when they are unable to borrow any they stand off to one side as spectators. Some witnesses later claimed that some of the men talked about leaving the ranks. The witnesses went on to say that Captain Parker rebuked them and threatened his men, telling them, "to stand fast, and not to fire on the British."

On the Lexington Green stands seventy-seven militia men with their weapons primed and ready to fire. For most of them the only thing they ever shot at is the occasional bird or squirrel. [Their training consisted of trying to march around without bumping into each other. They had practiced to load and fire fairly quickly. Of course, they never practiced while being fired at.]

They are farmers and shopkeepers by trade. All are God fearing men who sing and pray in church every week. They are husbands, fathers, sons, and brothers who are not looking for a fight. Six families make up twenty-nine of the militiamen, and there are a dozen father and son combinations. Two African Americans stand on the Lexington Green; Prince Estabrook a slave and Silas Burdoo a freeman.

As they stand there in the chilly morning air waiting for the sun to rise, they are aware they are about to face the best trained and best equipped army in the world. They know the soldiers they will face have killed before without thought or care. Each British foot soldier carries the feared seventeen inch long bayonet on their musket. This triangular shaped weapon does not cut through flesh, but rather it tears through it.

The small group of Americans stand on the Lexington Green straining to see down the road for the first sign of the British troops. As light begins to break through the dark sky, they can just make out the image of troops marching straight for them.

One witness later said that Captain Parker gave the order, "Stand your ground! Don't fire unless fired upon! But if they mean to have a war, let it begin here!" Before Paul Revere left to hide in the woods he recalls the order as having been, "Let the soldiers pass by. Do not molest them without they begin first."

Waiting for the British to advance are about seventy-seven armed men and off to the side are some 30 or 40 spectators watching. A few of the spectators are armed with muskets. Women and children peer out of windows in their homes at the unfolding event.

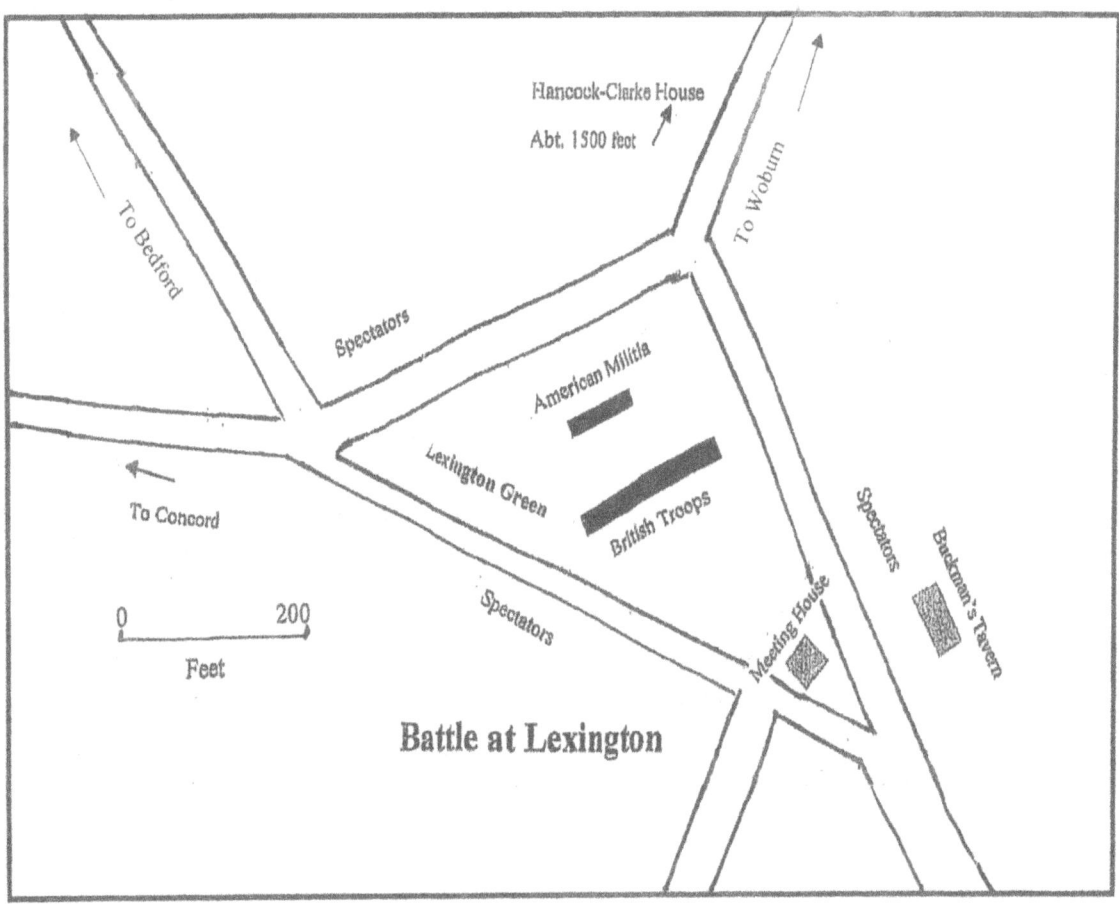

Battle at Lexington

PART II

ALARMS GIVEN TO OTHER TOWNS IN THE AREA

"There is an alarm. The Regulars are coming out; and if there is any soldier in the house he must run out and repair to Lexington as soon as possible."

----Rider giving the Lexington alarm in the town of Woburn.

During the night fleet messengers rode in every direction through the counties of Middlesex, Essex, and Norfolk counties. Everywhere there are cries of alarm, bells, and guns being fired to assemble the minutemen. All these men rush either to Lexington, Concord, or along the road from Boston to Concord. This will later be called Battle Road.

When alerted, each town sent riders to other towns with the alarm. The minutemen or militia of each town form and send their men out. When the men return home, many will enlist in the militia for a period of eight months and will participate in the Battle of Bunker Hill in June of 1775 and the Siege of Boston. After the fighting on the 19th of April, militias from New Hampshire, Rhode Island, and Connecticut began to arrive. Within days a militia army of over 15,000 men formed a siege line extending around Boston on three sides.

Listed here are some of the larger towns alerted that first night. Each town has its own story to tell.

Acton: The town is located twenty-one miles northwesterly from Boston and five miles west of Concord. The alarm is given early in the morning, and the men march to Concord about one a half hours away.

Francis Faulkner, Jr. is lying in bed and is awaked to the clatter of a horse drawing nearer and nearer. Suddenly he leaps from his bed and runs to his father's room shouting, "Father there's a horse coming on the full run, and he's bringing news!" His father also heard the horse and is already up, partly dressed, and with his gun in his hand.

The rider comes across the bridge and up to the house shouting, "Rouse your minutemen, Mr. Faulkner, the Regulars are marching on Lexington and Concord." As soon as the message is given the rider leaves to spread the news.

Captain Hunt and his company assemble at the home of Colonel Faulkner as arranged earlier. Also, women are there, ready to help. Stakes are driven into the lawn, kettles hung, fires built, and a dinner for the soldiers is soon cooking. Some of the older boys are delighted to carry the food in saddle bags to other soldiers. They are instructed that if the British are guarding the bridges, they should take the field roads. Colonel Faulkner soon marches his men to Concord, where he will take command of the Middlesex County Regiment which is assembling there.

The home of Captain Isaac Davis is about a mile west of the meetinghouse in the center of Acton, which is about six miles from the North Bridge in Concord. His company assembles, and the twenty men are anxious to march. Captain Davis remarks that he doesn't have a single man afraid to go. Davis seems particularly serious this morning. One of the men is speaking cheerily, and Davis gently criticizes the man. The Captain seems to have a premonition of his own fate, and wants to remind the others what the day may have in store for them.

As he and his men reach the road, Davis halts them and turns back toward his wife who is watching in the doorway of the house. He takes one last look at her and says, "Take good care of the children." He then marches away to Concord with his men.

[Many years later his wife Hannah said, "In the afternoon he was brought home a corpse. He was placed in my bedroom till the funeral. His countenance was pleasant, and seemed little altered."]

As the men march off to Concord the fifer Luther Blanchard and the drummer Francis Barker play the lively tune of the "White Cockade." This tune is also played in several other towns as the men march off. The song is of a young man who marches off to war with the promise that he will marry his girl when he returns. Here are the last two verses:

> "Then he took out his handkerchief to wipe my flowing eye,
>
> Leave off your lamentations likewise your mournful sighs.
>
> Leave off your grief and sorrow until I march o'er yon plain,
>
> We'll be married, we'll be married,
>
> In the springtime when I return again,
>
> My true love he is listed and it's all for him I'll rove,
>
> I'll write his name on every tree that grows in Yonder grove,
>
> My poor heart it does hallow, how my poor heart it does cry,
>
> To remind me, to remind me,
>
> Of my ploughboy, until the day I die."

Besides Isaac Davis, Abner Hosmer and James Hayward are killed and one man is wounded. Abner Hosmer is twenty-one years old and is a drummer who also carries a musket. Isaac dies at the North Bridge.

The following account is from a speech delivered in the House of Representatives of Massachusetts, February 3, 1851 by James T. Woodbury. He is requesting the town of Acton to build a monument over the remains of the three men that died on April 19, 1775.

"James Hayward was a twenty-five year old schoolteacher who had no business answering the call to Concord. He had been excused from military service because he had a crippled foot due to an accident with an ax years earlier. No one would have thought ill of him if he had stayed home the morning of April 19th, but he felt it his duty to answer the alarm. Since he was not a member of the company of minutemen he was not issued cartridges of powder and ball. Instead he carried loose powder in a powder horn."

"After fighting at Concord, James with the other men, chased after the British down the road while they were retreating. He reached the house of Ebenezer Fiske's house in Lexington and probably due to his handicap he stopped on the side of the road to rest. The British column had already passed so he was not concerned."

"Two British regulars emerged from the farm house and approached James. One of the men pointed his musket at the boy and said, "You're a dead man." James grabbed his musket and replied, "So are you." Both men fired at the same time. The British soldier fell dead. James was shot through the side and survived another very painful eight hours."

"James was eventually found by his father Deacon Samuel Hayward, who told the boy that the wound was fatal and did he regret answering the alarm. James weakly said, "Father, hand me my powder horn and bullet pouch. I started with one pound of powder and forty balls, you see what I have left, you see what I have been about. I never did such a forenoon's work before. Tell mother not to mourn too much for me for I am not sorry I turned out. I die willingly for my country. She will now, I doubt not, by the help of God, be free. And tell whom I loved better than my mother, you know who I mean, that I am not sorry. I shall never see her again. May I meet her in heaven.""

Note: This author wonders if the story of the death of James Hayward is factual or simply the embellishment of a man hoping to encourage some politicians to give some money for a worthy cause. If the story is not true, then it should be, because it typified the spirt of many of the patriots that fought that day.

****

Andover: The town is twenty-two miles north of Boston and eighteen miles northeast of Lexington. They receive the alarm about seven o'clock in the morning, and the minutemen are ready to march by ten a.m.

Colonel James Frye's oldest son is a farmer in the nearby town of Merrimack. When the alarm reaches him he is plowing his field. His wife knows he will lose no time to join the rest of the men, so she runs out of the house to tell him goodbye. She finds the oxen and plow standing there as her husband runs down the road. She runs after him and as she reaches the top of the hill he is almost out of sight. She gives him a loud call, and he turns, waves his hat and is soon gone.

As the men are on their way through Tewksbury about seven miles to the southwest, they learn that eight Americans had been killed at Lexington, and at Billerica they learn that the British are killing Americans at Concord. When they reach Bedford, they learn that the British are falling back from Concord.

Then, the nearly 200 men from Andover march at a fast pace to Cambridge hoping to catch the British there. They do not overtake the enemy but do see the straggling line of the fleeing, the wounded, and the dying left by the roadside. They also see the burning houses and ravaged farms on the road.

One soldier wrote in his diary that he saw a British soldier lying on the road with blood flowing from numerous holes in his body. He had been stabbed over and over by a passer-by.

Private James Stevens wrote in his journal, "that the Reglers was gainst Conkerd reached Andover at seven o'clock in the morning, and that Captain Poor's company gathered at the Meeting-house, and marched through Tewesbury & Billerica. We stopped to Polerds & eat some bisket & Ches on the common. At Lexington we came to the destruction of the Regelers. They killed eight of our men & shot a cannon ball through the metin-house. We went along through Lexington & we saw regerlers ded on the road & some of our men & three or fore houses was Burnt & some Hoses & hogs are kild, they plundered in every house they could get intp, they stove in windows & broke in tops of desks, we met the men a coming back very fast.."

When the men leave on the alarm, rumors begin to run through the remaining inhabitants of the town. There is a rumor that the regulars are coming to plunder the town. Valuables are packed, and some of the people are about to flee with them to the woods where they will hide and find shelter. Later, the word came that it was a false alarm. Years later a lady of North Andover said that her grandmother told her of the panic in one neighborhood.

****

Bedford: The town is fifteen miles northwest from Boston and nearly five miles northeast of Concord. Couriers, Benjamin Todd and Nathaniel Monroe, are sent from Lexington to give the alarm to Bedford. They ride to the home of Nathaniel Page in the morning shouting, "Up, Mr. Page, the regulars are out!"

Captain Cyrus Page later said," Our people were not surprised when the messenger reached us. We had seen Gage's men several times riding about town, and were kept familiar with the movements in Boston."

The minutemen gather around the fireplace in the tap room of the Fitch Tavern. Lydia Fitch serves them a breakfast of cornmeal mush and hot buttered rum. The Captain tells the men before they march on Concord, "It is a cold breakfast, boys, but we'll give the British a hot dinner; we'll have every dog of them." Over seventy men march on Concord this morning. When they arrive in Concord they help others in hiding the last remaining military supplies.

The alarm bell rings all day in Bedford, and the women busy themselves making meals for the men gathering at Concord. The women make sure the meals are delivered to the hungry men. News later reaches the town that Captain Jonathan Wilson was killed at Merriam's' Corner just a mile from Concord, and one man was wounded.

****

Brookline: The town is located four miles southwest of Boston and eleven miles southeast of Lexington. Three companies respond to the Lexington alarm. One company consists of ninety-four men under the command of Captain Thomas White. The other two companies are organized at the spur of the moment and consist of almost all the able-bodied of Brookline. The three companies set out for Lexington and travel no further than North Cambridge, when they meet the British who are retreating to Boston under Colonel Smith and Lord Percy.

The people of Brookline felt danger, when news came that Lord Percy with a detachment of 1,000 men would to pass near the town on their way to reinforce Colonel Smith at Lexington. Many of the families hastily pack blankets, provisions, what valuables they can collect on such short notice, and moved to the northern part of town where it might be safer.

The only person killed from Brookline was a graduate of Harvard, Isaac Gardner. His daughter later talked about his departure, "He went up to me and kissed me silently; then, as he reached the door, he turned and said, farewell." I said to him, "Oh Mr. Gardner, don't say that word. He again kissed me, and left home, never to return." When Isaac went to the meetinghouse he asked the wife of the Deacon to call upon his wife and comfort her.

Isaac Smith's dead body is found under an apple tree, and it contains so many wounds that the men did not want to bring it home during the day. His body is taken at night to Dr. Aspinwall's house, and the only family member to see the body is Isaac's oldest son. The next night the body is secretly buried, because the sight of the mangled body might lead to demonstrations towards the British in Boston. It is feared that these demonstrations might bring trouble upon the town.

****

Beverly: The town is located seventeen miles northeast of Boston. The men of the town answer the alarm and leave about ten o'clock to join the company of Captain Israel Hutchinson at Danvers. They fight on Battle Road near Boston. Reuben Kennison is seeding the fields when the alarm reaches him. He hurries home and meets his wife Apphia at the door of their home. She had heard the alarm and hands Reuben his old flintlock that is hanging over the fireplace. She hangs the powder horn over his shoulder. As Reuben runs down the road, he looks back and Apphia holds up her arm and bids him a long farewell.

Reuben is killed late in the day in the yard of Jason Russell in Menotomy. He is at the back of the house with other men behind a barricade made from shingles. The British come from behind them and a savage fight erupts. Reuben is struck in one area of his body by "a British bullet which pierced his breast, and was repeatedly, savagely bayoneted by the angry troops." His body is brought back home to Apphia in an ox cart. Three other men from town that fought near Reuben are wounded, and eleven other Americans are killed.

After the men had left Beverly that morning one woman remarked, "and none are left to protect us. If the regulars come during their absence, what will become of us, what shall we do?" Another woman spoke up, "Do? Who cares for the regulars? Let them come, and if they do not behave themselves, we'll take our brooms and drive them out of town."

****

Billerica: The town is about seventeen miles northwest from Boston and about nine miles northeast of Concord. They receive the alarm during the early morning, and the men gather at the Commons and then leave toward Concord. They go by way of Bedford, and fall in by the "Old Oak", where minutemen from Reading and other soldiers meet near Fitch's Tavern. They encounter the British at about twelve-thirty p.m. at Merriam's Corner about a mile outside of Concord as the British army begin their retreat. No one from Billerica is killed, and only two are wounded.

There were already some strong personal ill feelings about the British from the people of Billerica, because on March 8, 1775 a young man, Thomas Ditson, of Billerica was accused without a trial of trying to get a British soldier to desert. Thomas did this while in Boston, and he was seized by the British and kept prisoner until the next day. He was then taken out and was stripped, tarred, feathered, and dragged through the main streets. He was escorted by soldiers of the 7th regiment under the command of Colonel Nesbit to the music of Yankee Doodle. This outraged the town of Billerica.

****

Cambridge: The town is located three miles west of Boston. On the muster roll the minute men from Cambridge march on the alarm. [The number of miles they are credited with out and back home was twenty-eight miles.] They meet the retreating British outside Concord and harass them all the way back to Cambridge. There are seventy-seven men in the company under Captain Sam Thatcher. The fighting around Cambridge accounts for more than 1/3 of the patriots killed that day.

William Marcy, Moses Richardson, and John Hicks from Cambridge are killed. Moses Richardson is caught by surprise by British troops at Watson's Corner. This skirmish is in Cambridge when several patriots, Richardson being one, are hiding behind some barrels and are surprised by flanking British troops. Also, killed is William Marcy, a "simple-minded youth" sitting on a wall cheering, while thinking he is watching a parade.

****

Chelsea: The town is located a little over three miles northeast of Boston and too far away to get involved early in the alarm. The Rev. Samuel Phillips Payson is openly friendly to the Royal government, which leads to him being condemned by several of his patriotic minister friends. One of them, Rev. Treadwell, even refuses to exchange pulpits with him which is the custom. When Samuel hears the destruction and death done to his countrymen at Lexington, he becomes a supporter of the patriot cause.

Pastor Payson takes up his musket and leads the men in his congregation in attacking the retreating British at Menotomy. Pastor Payson and his men attack a party of twelve of the enemy who are carrying supplies they had looted. The rebels kill one British soldier and capture the rest. An account in the August 2, 1775 Pennsylvania Journal states:

> "The Rev. Mr. Payson, of Chelsea, in Massachusetts Bay, a mild, thoughtful, sensible man, at the head of a party of his own parish, attacked a party of regulars, killed some and took the rest prisoners. This gentleman has been hitherto on the side of government, but oppression having got to that pitch beyond which even a wise man cannot bear, he has taken up arms in defense of those rights, civil and religious, which cost their forefathers so dearly."

****

Chelmsford: The town is located twenty-three miles northwesterly of Boston and a little over eleven miles north of Concord. The alarm reaches the town on a warm morning before eight a.m. The guns fire and the drums beat as the men assemble. When Sergeant John Ford receives the news he leaves his mill outside of town to notify men along the Merrimack River. He quickly eats a bowl of bread and milk in his kitchen and [according to tradition] rides his horse to death while spreading the alarm.

Lieutenant Colonel Simeon Spaulding eats quickly and mounts his horse. His wife stands on a large rock in front of the house and gives him his gun and waves as he rides off. Many of the men working in their fields leave immediately upon hearing the alarm sound.

Samuel Parkhurst, age sixteen, calls out to his mother, "Mother, I hear the shouts, I'm going." [Later his descendants took great pride displaying a sword he took from a British officer at Ticonderoga.] Joseph Fletcher is just fourteen and cries when his mother refuses to let him go with the others. One young man, who is not a member of the minutemen, begs and obtains permission to go in the place of his elderly employer. He runs all the way to Concord by the side of Sergeant Ford's horse, while holding on to the stirrup strap.

As over 100 men prepare to leave, Parson Bridge requests that the men go to the meeting house and have prayers first. Sergeant Ford replies that they have more urgent business at hand and leaves with his men.

Captain Moses Parker's Company, and Captain Oliver Barron's Company march, in squads, rather than in regular order. They reach Concord and come into it at Meriam's Corner and on Harsy's Hill in time for the pursuit. Most of the men reach Concord before noon and encounter the British at Meriam's Corner. Only two men from Chelmsford are wounded.

****

Danvers: The town is located sixteen miles north of Boston and twenty miles northeast of Lexington. The alarm is given around nine in the morning and the rider does not want to dismount, but he calls in a loud voice as he gallops along, "There's a battle at Lexington! We have met the Regulars! Hurry to help!"

Captain Asa Prince and Captain Samuel Flint gather the men from the village, while other Captains gather their men from the Plains, New Mills, Beverly, Putnamville, and Beaver Brook. A total of 303 men rush to meet the British. They start at about ten a.m. and reach Menotomy at about three in the afternoon. There they fight the retreating British in a bloody battle. The town will have seven men killed, two wounded, and one missing.

That night a sorrowful group congregate in Colonel Hutchinson's house at New Mills to wait for the news from the battle. There are women there whose husbands had seen battle in the old wars and knew what a dreadful battle meant. The young women, born and raised in peace, and the little children are clinging to the older children anticipating what is about to happen.

Late into the night several men on horseback ride up to the house escorting a horse-cart, which contains the dead patriots. On the kitchen floor of the house the dead are unrolled from the bloody sheets and the next morning they will be taken away for burial. This is repeated in many towns that night.

The dead include Henry Jacobs age twenty-two, Samuel Cook age thirty-three, Ebenezer Goldthwait age twenty-one, George Southwick age twenty-five, Benjamin Daland, Jr. age twenty-five, Jotham Webb age twenty-two, and Perely Putnam age twenty-two. All the men died at, or near the Jason Russell house. Two other men were wounded and one was missing.

****

Dedham: The town is ten miles southwest of Boston. The alarm reaches them a little after nine in the morning by way of Needham and Dover. They have five companies of militia with a total of 202 men. Aaron Guild, a Captain in the British Army during the French and Indian War, is plowing his fields in South Dedham when he hears the alarm. He immediately "left plough in furrow and oxen standing" to leave for the conflict, and he arrives in time to fire upon the retreating British.

Farmers stop what they are doing and join the fight. Illustration, National Archives.

Captain Joseph Guild leads the minutemen, and on the road he meets a man who says the alarm is false. The Captain seizes the man with his own hand, gags him, and leaves him under the charge of some of his men, lest the report should reach more willing ears and be believed. The men from Dedham fight at Battle Road. Elias Haven age thirty is killed in Cambridge, and one other man from town is wounded.

****

Framingham: The town is twenty miles southwesterly from Boston. They receive the alarm before eight in the morning. The alarm bell is rung, and guns fire, which assemble many of the three companies of militia. Captain Simon Edgell, Captain Micajah Gleason, and Captain Jesse Eames march their companies out by ten a.m. Those living in the extreme south and west parts of town follow a little later.

Not long after the men leave, a report is spread that Negroes are coming to massacre everyone in town. This seems more frightening to the women and children because of the absence of nearly all the able-bodied men. Nobody stops to ask where the hostile Negroes are coming from, because all the Negroes in the area are patriots. It is probably a lingering memory of an earlier

Indian alarm. The wife of Captain Edgell and the other women take axes, pitchforks, and clubs into their homes and securely bolt the doors. For those defenseless ones at home it is a terrible day.

The men march through Sudbury to Lincoln and join other patriots taking the high ground at Brook's Hill. This hill overlooks the road that the British are using to retreat. They inflict heavy causalities on the English and force their troops to charge up the hill, so that the main British column can pass. British Ensign Henry De Berniere later wrote, "All the hills on each side of us were covered with rebels…so that they kept the road always lined and a very hot fire on us without intermission." This Ensign just six weeks previously had dismissed the Framingham minutemen as amateurs.

Ebenezer Hemenway shoots a British soldier named Thomas Sowers near Merriam's Corner in Concord and takes his gun home as a souvenir. Noah Eaton is loading his musket behind a rise, when a British soldier stands before him and starts to reload his own gun. Thinking quickly Noah raises his unloaded musket, and he points it toward the British soldier demanding him to surrender. Later, the Englishman realizes that he had been captured with an unloaded weapon. No one from Framingham is killed that day and only one man wounded.

****

Groton: The town is thirty-four miles northwest from Boston. The alarm is received in the morning, but the two companies of over 100 men minutemen are too late to catch up with the British retreat. [The men will get their chance to fight at Bunker Hill that June.]

In late afternoon of the 18th a meeting is called for the minutemen. Some brass cannons had arrived in Groton from Concord. Sensing there might be trouble in Concord it is suggested that the minute men be sent there. Not all are in agreement, so only nine men leave for Concord that evening. In around six hours they travel the seventeen miles during the middle of the night carrying lit pine torches. They reach Concord early in the morning in time for the fight.

****

Lincoln: The town is fourteen miles northwest of Boston and four miles southeast of Concord. Dr. Samuel Prescott escapes the British soldiers that captured Paul Revere, and warns Concord. His brother Abel rides to the south to warn Sudbury, Farmingham, and Lincoln. The rider misses the road that leads to Captain William Smith of the Lincoln minutemen company. Mary Hartwell is enlisted to bring the word to the Captain.

Mary returns home to prepare breakfast for her husband Samuel Hartwell and his brothers. They eat, and Mary watches as her husband and his brothers ride off to join the minutemen. [Many years later she told her grandchildren, "I knew what all that meant, and I feared that I should never see your grandfather again."]

Samuel Farrar, a Lieutenant in Smith's Company, leaves his farm, and his wife Mary becomes terrified that the British will burn their home. She turns the cattle loose, grabs her baby, takes the family Bible, a looking glass, and the family silverware to the woods a half a mile away. There she waits in dread for what the day would bring.

The Lincoln men reach Concord a little before the sun comes up. As dawn breaks the men wait for the approaching British.

****

Littleton: The town is located twenty-eight miles northwest from Boston and eleven miles east of Concord. The alarm sounds in the early morning and the minutemen muster at Liberty Square on the south side of town. They march to the Old North Bridge just in time to fight the British.

****

Lynn: The town lies ten miles north of Boston and a little over sixteen miles east of Lexington. The people receive the alarm early in the morning, and many of the men immediately leave for Lexington without waiting to be organized, and with any weapon they can find. One man has no other equipment than a long fowling piece (shotgun) without a bayonet, a horn of powder, and a seal-skin pouch filled with bullets and buck shot. The men walk to Lexington in less than six hours and are waiting for the British as they retreat through Lexington.

Abednego Ramsdell age twenty-five has gone out early that morning. He kills a couple of black ducks, and as he is returning home he hears the alarm. He drops the birds and starts running to his home. He is seen running through town with his stockings falling over his shoes. He arrives at Lexington in the middle of the day. He is later killed in Menotomy. Three others from Lynn will be killed; Daniel Townsend, William Flint, and Thomas Hadley. Also two men are wounded and one is missing.

An account of Daniel Townsend's death is found in the book *Townsend-Townsend, 1066-1909*. Daniel's wife never recovers from the shock of his death, and she dies later in October.

Timothy Monroe, a wounded survivor and witness recounts, "that he was standing behind a house with Daniel Townsend, firing on the British troops as they were coming down the road on their retreat toward Boston. Townsend had just fired, and exclaimed, 'There's another red-coat down,' when Monroe, looking around, saw to his astonishment that they were completely hemmed in by the flank guard of the British army, who were coming down through the field behind them. They immediately ran into the house and sought for the cellar, but no cellar was there. All this time, which was indeed but a moment, the balls were pouring through the back window, making havoc of the glass. Townsend leaped through the end window, carrying the sash and all with Him, and instantly fell dead. Monroe followed him and escaped." Daniel had been shot seven times. His body was carried back to Lynn.

****

Malden: The town is five miles north of Boston. Early in the morning a rider comes along the Medford Road yelling, "The regulars are out!" The meeting house bell is rung, and the minutemen begin to assemble. They are ordered by Colonel Thomas Gardner to march to Watertown about eight miles away and west of Boston. As they march from Kettell's Tavern out of town, women and children march with them to the beat of Winslow Sergeant's drum.

When they reach Medford, they are met by an officer who stops them and tells them to wait until they hear some news about the British. About noon they are told to go to Menotomy with the intention of cutting off the retreating British troops.

After the men had left, the women filled saddle-bags with food and dispatched Israel Cook to ride after them with the food. Israel meets the retreating British on the road, and they kill his horse. He shoulders the saddle-bags and wanders around, until he meets his friends who are in need of food.

One of several men who left early is John Edmunds, who lives on the northeast part of town. A boy named Breeden, about eighteen years old and unarmed, says he will get a gun if they will let him go with them. Later in the day when they are following the retreating British troops, the boy becomes so daring that Phineas Sprague, a minuteman, remarks that he will probably be killed.

The boy sees one British solder lagging behind so he borrows a gun and follows the soldier. When the others come up, they see that Breeden has killed the British soldier and is eating the man's rations.

****

Medford: The town is located about five and a half miles from Boston and fourteen miles east of Concord. Before midnight Paul Revere rides across the bridge into Medford, stops at the door of Captain Isaac Hall, and gives the alarm. Around sixty men march to Concord to wait for the British.

Henry Putnam, sixty-five years old, is exempt from military duty due to his age. But he will not remain home when fighting is to be done, so he grabs his musket and joins the march. [He is later killed in battle.]

Rev. Edward Brooks rides on horseback to Concord and is in the battle at the North Bridge. Lieutenant Edward Thornton Gould, a British soldier, is wounded in that fight. Rev. Brooks saves the man's life and brings him back to Medford as a prisoner. Later Edward T. Gould says in sworn testimony, "I am now treated with the greatest humanity and taken all possible care of by the provincials at Medford."

One other man from Medford is killed that day. William Polly, age eighteen, is shot by the British, while he rode on his horse a distance from the main road in Menotomy. He dies of the wound on April 25, 1775.

****

Menotomy: The town is six and a half miles northwest of Boston. Paul Revere spreads the alarm to the town at the start of his ride. As the British retreat the next day, they pass through Menotomy again and more blood is shed there than at Lexington and Concord combined. In all twenty-five Americans are killed there as well as forty British troops. Minutemen from surrounding towns converge there as the British retreat.

Benjamin Locke and fifty-two minutemen assemble on the green by the meeting house, after the British march through from Boston early on the 19th. They march to the aid of Lexington and fight the retreating British. Women and children are sent away to a place of safety. Many people hide their silver and other valuables, expecting that when the army returns there will be murder and plunder.

The men from Menotomy that die this day are Jason Russell, Jabez Wyman, and Jason Winship. There is also one man wounded and two missing. Later in the day the alarm is given, because the British are retreating and will pass through Menotomy on the road in front of Jason Russell's house.

Jason, fifty-eight years old, stays behind but sends his family to safety saying, "An Englishman's house is his castle." Jason Russell, Jabez Wyman, Jason Winship, and other minutemen, hide in the yard waiting to ambush the British. Another column of British are marching along the ridge behind the house, so as the battle begins the minutemen are caught between the two British columns. Jabez Wyman and Jason Winship are killed in the battle. Jason Russell runs to get inside his house, but because he is lame he cannot outrun the British troops. He is bayonetted in his own doorway.

****

Needham: The town is located twelve miles southwest of Boston. The news reaches Bullard's Tavern about nine in the morning, and Ephraim Bullard sounds the alarm by firing his gun on Bullard's Hill. In remote parts of Needham the minutemen are summoned by the blare of a trumpet blown by the slave Abel Benson.

The men meet at the minister's house, because the ammunition is kept there in the cellar in a large brick chimney closet. The women run to the tavern and begin molding bullets. Nearly forty men serve this day under the command of Captain Caleb Kingsbury, and they are paid a penny a mile to and from their homes. The militia stops at Watertown about seven and a half miles away, and they reach Menotomy in time to harass the British troops on their retreat.

Lieutenant John Bacon hears the alarm early and rides his horse seven miles to Newton. Once there he sends his horse back home. It is another eight miles walking distance to Watertown the arranged meeting place. People later said of him, "He was the most impatient off all to get on to the battle."

On Battle Road patriots between the flanking British troops and the main body are trapped. John Bacon is killed by this group along with Amos Mills, Elisha Mills, Nathaniel Chamberlain, and Jonathan Parker. Two other men are wounded.

John and his friend "Old Hawes" are lying behind a wall when Hawes suddenly hollers, "Run or you're dead, here's the guard!" As they run Bacon is shot near the third button of his waistcoat. Elisha Mills steps out of a barn to fire at the enemy, and he is shot several times. Jonathan Parker is surprised at West Cambridge by a flank guard at a barn and is shot attempting to reach the woods. [There are five men from Needham killed that day and two wounded.]

****

Newton (Newtown): The town is located eight miles westerly from Boston. The alarm is received at early dawn by a volley from one of John Pigeon's field guns that he keeps at the gun house in Newton Centre, near the church.

A company of minutemen meet on the parade ground but no officers are present. Michael Jackson is chosen leader, steps forward, and orders the men to march. They leave for Watertown three miles north and about one hour away. When they arrive at Watertown several officers are with a group of men holding a meeting around the schoolhouse. Michael listens to them for a while and feels it is time to get in the fight rather than stand around talking. He says to the men, "Not now the wag of the tongue, but the pull of the trigger." He tells them he intends to take his company the shortest route to get a shot at the British. Some men join Michael's company, and they march off to Concord twelve miles away. In about three hours they come in contact with Lord Percy's troops near Concord.

One old veteran cannot be forced to stay home because he says, "I want to see what the boys are doing." During the fight he is shot through the hand, which he binds up with his handkerchief. He brings home the gun of a British soldier who fell in battle. A total of 218 minute men from town fight that day, and only one is wounded.

****

Pepperell: The town is early thirty-nine miles northwesterly from Boston, and the alarm reaches them about nine in the morning.

It is twenty-one miles northwest of Concord, and it will take about seven hours by foot. General Prescott gives orders to the Pepperell and Hollis companies to march to Groton, about one and a half hours southeast and join others of the regiment. The Pepperell Company receives the alarm much later than the company in Groton, but they organize and march so quickly that they reach Groton parade ground before the Groton companies are ready. So, they halt for a few minutes and then march off without them.

When they get to Concord, the British have already left. So, they march toward Cambridge but are unable to overtake the British. It is nearly fifteen miles from Concord to Cambridge and over a four hour walk. [The men later get their chance to fight at Bunker Hill.]

David Wright leaves with the minutemen and leaves his thirty-five year old wife Prudence behind. She overhears some local Tories, who are friendly to the British, discussing plans to send messages between the British in the north and the British in Boston. She realizes that the road the Tories will take between the north and Boston passes through the town of Pepperell.

Prudence calls to arms the thirty to forty women remaining in town. The women dress in their men's clothing and gather weapons, and they elect Prudence as the commander of their militia company. Prudence chooses seventeen year old Sarah Hartwell Shattuck as her lieutenant, and the newly formed company stands ready for a fight. They are armed with muskets, pitchforks, and any other tool that can be used as a weapon.

The women gather at the bridge over the Nashua River, which is just outside of Pepperell on the road to Hollis. The women guard the bridge, patrol the road, and swear that no enemy of freedom will pass that bridge. The company of women become known as the Prudence Wright Guard. They hope that if British troops show up, that they can scare the troops off before it is discovered that the patriots facing them are women.

The bridge is located out in the country with no homes nearby. The road to the bridge curves around an area of high ground, so that if you are traveling from the north the bridge cannot be seen until you are nearly on it. The women wait all night in silence watching for the enemy. Late in the night two riders approach the bridge, and Prudence jumps out in front of them and shines her lantern into their eyes. She demands to know who they are and what business they are on. When the startled men try to escape, the company of women surround them and grab the reins of their horses.

One rider, Captain Leonard Whiting, is a well know Tory in the area, and he draws his pistol and is about to fire it. The other rider, also a Tory, is Samuel Cummings who is the brother of Prudence. Samuel tells the captain to lower his weapon, when he recognizes his sister's voice. He tells the captain that his sister, "would wade through blood for the rebel cause." The two men dismount, and when they are searched, dispatches from the British troops in the north to the British in Boston are found in Samuel's boot. The prisoners are taken to a local home and guarded the rest of the night. In the morning the women take their prisoners to Groton and turn them over to the Committee of Safety.

****

Reading: The town is thirteen miles north from Boston alarm and ten miles northeast of Lexington. Guns are fired just before sunrise to give the alarm to the townspeople.

When they first hear the alarm the men run to find what arms and ammunition they can grab and then begin to march. Reuben Eaton likes to hunt and proceeds to clean his gun, supply his lock with a new flint, fill his horn with powder, and puts bullets in a pouch. He then gathers other equipment, and when prepared he follows in pursuit. He reaches Concord in time to join the skirmish there.

****

Roxbury: This is the adjoining town to Boston and is the first town in that direction to learn of the British movement. William Dawes, the first messenger out of Boston, passes through the town on his round-about-way to Lexington, and the alarm is delivered before eleven p.m.

Three companies under the command of Captain Moses Whiting, Captain William Draper, and Captain Lemuel Child take an active part on the 19th. As they march toward the British forces, many women and children flee to other towns for greater safety. Mrs. Greaton takes her younger children, articles that she is able to carry in a cart, and flees to Brookline.

****

Salem: The town is a little over fourteen miles northeast of Boston. On the way to Menotomy Colonel Timothy Pickering and more than 300 militia men from the county of Essex meet at two taverns to engage the retreating British. When they finally do arrive, Pickering decides not to fight the British, which enables them to reach Boston. The only man from Salem that is killed is Benjamin Pierce, who is shot dead around the Russell House in Menotomy.

****

Shirley: The town is thirty-six miles northwest of Boston. One of the men who tries to join is William Longley, who is bent with age. When reminded of his age and physical condition he says, "True, I cannot handle a musket, yet I will fight the red-coats with my two canes." The town send eighty men to Concord and then to Cambridge, but they are unable to overtake the retreating British. The men later got their chance to fight at Bunker Hill.

****

Stow: The town is twenty-five miles west of Boston. Before April 19th the colonists fear the British might seize the arms in Concord, so they move some of the supplies to Stow. A cannon is hidden in the surrounding woods, and gunpowder and other supplies are hidden at the meeting house and in a small powder house on Pilot Grove Hill. When the alarm reaches Stow the minutemen assemble in the early morning hours. A total of eighty-one men march to Concord and fight the British at the "Bloody Angle." [This is where Battle Road makes a sharp turn.] They pursue the British along Battle Road and, suffer only one man wounded.

****

Sudbury: The town is nineteen miles west of Boston. The news is received by a messenger, from Concord eight miles away, who reports to Thomas Plympton, a member of the Provincial Congress. Captain Nixon is aroused between four and five o'clock in the morning by a messenger shouting, "Up, up! The redcoats are as far as Concord."

Two companies from the west side of the town go by the road through North Sunbury, and the men of the east side go by way of Lincoln. While marching they are ordered to go to the North Bridge at Concord. Captain Nixon starts off at once on horseback, takes his men, and marches on to the North Bridge in Concord. Strains of the tune "The White Cockade" can be heard as they march. Along the route mothers, wives, and children appear hoping to catch a glimpse of a loved one. Many years later a young girl said her grandmother told her that she put her ear to the ground and could hear the sounds of distant gunfire.

Deacon Josiah Haynes, age seventy-nine, is killed as the British retreat through Lexington. Asahel Reed is also killed and 1 man is wounded.

****

Tewksbury: The town is twenty miles northwest of Boston and thirteen miles north of Lexington. The alarm is given about two in the morning with the rider shouting, "The Regulars are on the way to Concord and I have alarmed all the towns from Charlestown to here." The alarm awakens Captain John Trull, who fires three shots from his bedroom window to arouse General Varnum across the Merrimack River in Dracut. The men march to Concord and fight the British at Merriam's Corner. Trull and his men harass the British all the way back to Charlestown.

Many years later one of Trull's minutemen, Eliphalet Manning, told one of Trull's grandchildren the following story, "I fought with your grandfather from Concord to Charlestown. He would cry out to us as we sheltered ourselves behind the trees: 'Stand trim, or the Rascals will shoot your elbows off.'"

****

Westford: The town is twenty-six miles northwest of Boston. Samuel Prescott alerts sixty-eight Westford minutemen who march to Concord ten miles away and fight.

****

Woburn: The town is ten miles northwest of Boston and a little over five miles northeast of Lexington. Mr. Douglas is awaked about an hour before sunrise by a knock at the door and a man shouting, "There is an alarm. The Redcoats are coming out; and if there is any soldier in the house he must run out and repair to Lexington as soon as possible."

Douglass with others hurry to Lexington nearly two hours away by foot, but they arrive too late for the opening battle. They then walk to Tanner's Brook near Lincoln and wait for the British to return later in the afternoon. Some of the men stay home to protect their families or take them to places of safety.

During the fight with the British in Lincoln the town of Woburn suffers two men killed, two wounded, and one missing. Daniel Thompson and the rest of the men from Woburn are on either side of Bedford Road in Lincoln, which is just a few miles from Concord. When the British arrive, Daniel takes cover behind a barn and begins firing. A British soldier sneaks up behind him and shoots him in the back. The British soldier is killed at once by another minuteman. Daniel lays dead at the age of forty. Daniel's brother Abijah carries Daniel back to his wife and children.

Asahel Porter age twenty-three is returning home from Boston earlier that morning and is taken prisoner by the British troops. He attempts to escape during the Battle of Lexington and is shot.

Two days before the battle the town voted to raise a number of minutemen not to exceed fifty men. They were to meet half a day every week each month from May to October for instruction in the *"military science of handling the firelock."* The town also voted to pay each man a dollar if called into service.

****

Worcester: The town is located thirty miles southwest of Concord. The people receive the alarm before noon by a messenger mounted on a white horse dripping with sweat, and bloody from spurring. Driving at full speed through the town he shouts, "To arms, to arms! The war has begun!"

At the church the horse falls exhausted. Another is procured and the news is sent on. The bell rings out the alarm, cannons are fired, and a special messenger is dispatched to every part of the town to summon the soldiers. In a little while 110 men, under Captain Timothy Bigelow, are paraded on the Green and soon march to Concord. They are met on the way by news of the British retreat, so they change their course toward Boston.

Marching to the fight   Lithograph by Currier & Ives, 1876.   Library of Congress

PART III

THE BATTLE OF LEXINGTON

"I have trained them. They would fight, and if need be die, too, under the shadow of the house of God."

----Pastor Clarke, when asked just before the battle if his men would fight.

Leading up to the Lexington Battle:

As the British approach Concord the road comes to a fork. Lieutenant Jesse Adair is at the head of the advance guard, and he decides to turn right toward Bedford. This will lead the troops onto the Lexington Common where the Americans are assembled. The left road bypasses the Common and would take the British to Concord. Major Pitcairn sees the mistake, and he rapidly rides to the advance guard. He arrives too late to stop the unfolding events from taking place.

As the Americans wait for the British, Pastor Clarke is asked if the men from his congregation will fight. His reply is stern, "I have trained them. They would fight, and if need be die, too, under the shadow of the house of God."

As the sun starts to break on the horizon there is a light westerly wind and the morning temperature is around forty-six degrees. The afternoon temperature will rise to a very comfortable fifty-six degrees. It is another beautiful morning in Massachusetts, and for some soldiers on both sides it will be their last sunrise.

5:00 a.m. April 19, 1775

Back in Boston: General Gage receives the message from Lieutenant Colonel Francis Smith requesting reinforcements.

Lexington: Captain Parker does not realize that his drum and alarm guns are taken as a challenge by the advancing British officers. One of the captured American scouts tells Major Pitcairn that there are 500 militiamen waiting for him in Lexington. As the sun rises Pitcairn orders his men to double their ranks, load their muskets, and move toward town in a double-time march.

Pitcairn is expecting hundreds of militiamen to oppose him in Lexington. He feels very relieved to see a group of farmers opposing him. He thinks it will be an easy task to disarm the colonists, since he has little respect for the armed citizens. Weeks before he had said, "I am satisfied that one active campaign, a smart action, and burning two or three of their towns, will set everything to rights." He would later be killed at Bunker Hill by a former slave Peter Salem.

For the moment the British force of about 400 troops and the American force of about seventy men face each other separated by about fifty yards. Neither side wants to open fire and be the aggressor. Major Pitcairn remembers his orders are to destroy the stores at Concord and not to molest the inhabitants in the area. However, he cannot leave these Americans armed and possibly later taking shots at his men. He decides that he will position his men to surround the Americans and disarm them. He did not want to capture them, because he has no way to take care of this many prisoners.

Captain Parker realizes how outnumbered he is and how futile it would be to resist. He orders his men to file away. In all the noise and confusion the men may not have heard Parker, for they stand their ground. Pitcairn gives orders to press forward and surround the militia.

British Lieutenant Sutherland later wrote, "I heard Major Pitcairn call out, 'Soldiers, don't fire, keep your ranks, form and surround them.'"

Major Pitcairn shouts to the rebels, "Lay down your arms, you damned rebels and disperse!" The Americans do not respond to his command so he again shouts, "Damn you, why don't you lay down your arms?"

A few of the Americans start to move away, but they are slow to respond to the command from the Major. Pastor Clarke later wrote, "…many of them not so speedily as they might have done." They are not military men who are trained to react as a unit. The men that do move away carry their weapons with them. No one leaves their weapon as ordered by the British.

Suddenly a single shot rings out. The British troops, now about forty yards away, respond with a volley. When the British open fire none of the Americans are hit, and they believe that the first British volley is just powder and no shot. The first volley goes over the heads of the militiamen.

When the British fires a second volley some Americans begin to fall. John Munroe recalls, "Seeing no one fall I said to my relative, Ebenezer Munroe, Jr., that they had fired nothing but powder." On the second discharge, Ebenezer replied, "They have fired something besides powder now, for I am wounded in the arm."

Battle of Lexington, New York Public Library's Digital Library.

Major Pitcairn orders his men to stop firing, but they pay no attention to him. After the second volley is fired by the British, they level their bayonets and charge the militiamen. As the militiamen begin to retreat from the Common, several halt and return fire.

Mrs. Lydia Hancock leaves the Hancock-Clarke house and is outside to see what is going on, when a British bullet whizzes by her head and hits the barn. "What was that?" she exclaims. She is told to take care of herself.

William Tidd is pursued by an officer who cries out to him, "Stop, or you are a dead man." William springs over a pair of bars, fires once, and makes his escape. John Tidd stays too long on the Common and is struck by the cutlass of an officer on horseback. As he lies on the ground he is robbed of all his belongings and left for dead. He recovers and lives for many years after that memorable day.

John Munroe fires and then retreats a couple of yards. He loads a second time with two balls and fires, but the charge is too heavy and he loses about a foot from the muzzle end of his gun. Jedediah Munroe receives a wound that morning and is killed in the afternoon.

Solomon Brown, after the second volley from the British, fires at them from the back door of Buckman's Tavern. In order to get a better shot at them, he goes to the front door and fires from there. The British fire back at him several times. John Buckman the tavern owner fusses at Solomon for using his building as a fort, so Solomon runs out and hides behind a stone wall and opens fire again.

Elijah Sanderson later wrote, "Some Tories, who wouldn't stand up for their country and reckoned the British brothers, had stood at the tavern door to watch the soldiers' advance."

Dorothy Quincy who is looking out the window later says, "Two men were being brought into the house. One, whose head had been grazed by a ball, insisted that he was dead; but the other, who was shot in the arm, behaved better."

Scattered firing on both sides continues as the Americans leave the field. After the firing stops and the Americans combatants flee, Pastor Clarke surveys the green by his church. He sees eight of his congregation dead. Pastor Clarke later said, "From this day, will be dated the liberty of the world."

The British soldiers have broken ranks during the charge and are about to start breaking into houses when Lt. Colonel Smith arrives. Pitcairn and Smith soon get the troops under control and reform the men into columns. Smith finds a drummer and orders him to beat assembly. After every one calms down and order is soon restored, the infantry is given permission to fire a victory volley and give three cheers. While the British are cheering their victory, the townspeople are standing over their dead friends.

After the firing stops the British troops then laugh, and damn the Yankees, and joke that the Americans cannot bear the smell of gunpowder. Soon the cheering stops and the British troops begin to assemble for their march to Concord.

Joshua Simond is in charge of the stock of ammunition in the upper gallery of the Lexington meeting house. He is in there filling powder-horns when the British come into town. As the horns are filled, the men quickly carry them downstairs. One of the last to leave the house is Caleb Harrington, who is shot as he leaves the meeting house. Joshua and one other person are left in the house. After the firing stops, a British officer comes up to the house and orders, "Clear that house." Joshua and his companion hide on one side of the room. Joshua is determined to blow up the house rather than be captured. He cocks his pistol and places the muzzle upon an open keg of powder as the soldiers start to come up the steps. He hears an order to halt given and then a right about. The soldiers leave the house, and they start to march to Concord.

The causalities for the day are for the Americans, eight men killed and ten wounded. One wounded man is the slave Prince Estabrook, the first African American wounded in the Revolution. He later served in the army and gained his freedom.

For the British there are two wounded. One British soldier Private Johnson who will later be killed at Bunker Hill is shot in the thigh, and another man is wounded in the hand. Pitcairn's horse is wounded twice.

****

These are men who died at Lexington in the first battle of the Revolution:

1. **Jonathon Harrington** was fatally wounded by a musket ball and crawled back to his home. His wife and eight year old son were at the window and saw him crawling across the road to their home. She came outside to help him and he died at her feet.
2. **Caleb Harrington,** who had been sent to the meeting house before the battle to obtain a quantity of powder stored there, was attempting to escape from the meeting house when he was shot and killed.
3. **Jonas Parker** was wounded and was attempting to reload after firing his first shot. He frequently had said, "I will never run from British troops." Jonas was bayoneted to death as he faced the enemy. Having loaded his musket he put his hat on the ground between his feet, which contained his ammunition He was wounded at the enemy's second fire, sank to his knees, discharged his musket, and while loading was run through by a bayonet thrust.
4. **Isaac Muzzy** who had arrived with his father was killed on the Green near where the line was formed.
5. **Robert Munroe** was bayonetted on the Green near where the line was formed. He was the oldest to die at the age of sixty-three. He was by the wall at Merriam's barn. His daughter Anna and two sons Ebenezer and John must have witnessed his death.
6. **John Brown** was killed off the Green.
7. **Samuel Hadley** was killed off the Green.
8. **Asahel Porter** had been taken prisoner on the march to Lexington and saw a chance to escape, and he was shot near the Green. He was cautioned to walk away not run. So, when he began to run he was shot. Another prisoner Josiah Richardson walked away and escaped safely.

Questions raised after the battle:

After the battle there were inquiries on both sides as to what happened. There were three questions that needed answers; were the Americans dispersing when fired upon, did they return fire, and who fired first? Each side had a different version of the events.

There was no doubt that the Americans did return fire. Accounts on both sides bear this out, plus the British had two wounded soldiers.

Were the Americans dispersing when fired upon? A British soldier he recalled in a letter, "Colo. Smyth of the 10th ordered us to rush on them with our Bayonets fixed; at which time some of the Peasants fired on us, and our then returning the fire, the Engagement began." According to this soldier's account the Americans fired first and were not dispersing.

Joseph Underwood testified on March 7, 1825, "When the British were moving toward the colonists some of the men on seeing them started to back off. Captain Parker gave the order for every man to stand his ground, and he said he would order the first man shot that offered to leave his post. I stood very near Captain Parker when the Regulars came up, and am confident he did not order his men to disperse till the British troops had fired upon us the second time."

Captain John Parker testified, "I ordered our Militia to meet on the Common in said Lexington to consult what to do, and concluded not to be discovered, nor meddle or make with said Regular Troops (if they should approach) unless they should insult or molest us; and, upon their sudden Approach, I immediately ordered our Militia to disperse, and not to fire:— Immediately said Troops made their appearance and rushed furiously, fired upon, and killed eight of our Party without receiving any Provocation therefor from us."

The British gave their version of who fired first: Major Pitcairn said he was turning to tell his men to disarm the colonists when he thought he saw a gun from behind a wall flash in the pan. Some witnesses among the regulars reported the first shot was fired by a colonial onlooker, who was behind a hedge or around the corner of a tavern.

Many of the British troops said the first shot came behind a hedge or stone wall. Some say from Buckman's Tavern. There was even talk that someone acting under the orders of Samuel Adams fired the first shot.

The Americans gave their version of who fired first: According to Paul Revere and other witness the first shot was from a pistol. The British officers were the only ones likely to have pistols. Paul Revere heard and saw the shot, but was unable to tell who fired it. Revere knew Major Pitcairn well and knew that he did not fire the opening shot.

Benjamin Tidd and Joseph Abbott testified in 1775, "The regulars fired, first a few guns which we took to be pistols, from some of the regulars who were mounted on horses." A deposition taken at Lexington April 25, 1775 by several minutemen that were present stated, ".....some of our company were coming to the parade, with their backs towards the troops, and others on the parade began to disperse, when the regulars fired on the company, before a gun was fired by any of our company on them."

A spectator named Timothy Smith said, "I saw the regular fire before on the Lexington Company before a gun was fired by any of our company on the regulars." Some observers reported a mounted British officer firing first. Both sides generally agreed that the initial shot did not come from the men on the ground immediately facing each other.

On the One Year Anniversary of the Battle of Lexington, Pastor Clarke preached a sermon based upon his eyewitness testimony of the event. He called his sermon, The Fate of Blood-Thirsty Oppressors and God's Tender Care of His Distressed People. He added this narrative to his printed sermon, "So far from firing first upon the King's troops, upon the most careful enquiry, it appears that but a very few of our people fired upon the troops, they were wounded themselves, or saw others killed, or wounded by them; and looking upon it as next to impossible for them to escape."

Participant-observers in Massachusetts sent the following depositions to the Second Continental Congress concerning what they saw at Lexington and Concord. The original document is from the Journals of the Continental Congress.

Lexington, April 25, 1775:

"I, Elijah Sanderson, above named, do further testifie and declare, that I was on Lexington Common, the Morning of the Nineteenth of April, aforesaid, having been dismissed by the Officers abovementioned, and saw a Large Body of Regular Troops advancing toward Lexington Company, many of whom were then dispersing. I heard one of the Regulars, whom I took to be an officer, say, "Damn them, we will have them," and immediately the Regulars shouted aloud, Run and fired upon the Lexington Company, which did not fire a Gun before the Regulars Discharged on them; Eight of the Lexington Company were killed while they were dispersing, and at a Considerable Distance from each other, and Many wounded, and altho' a spectator, I narrowly Escaped with my Life."

Affidavit No. 2. Lexington, April 23, 1775:

"I, Thomas Rice Willard, of lawful age, do Testify and Declare, that being in the House of Daniel Harrington, of said Lexington, on the Nineteenth Instant, in the morning, about half an hour before sunrise, looked out at the window of said house, and saw (as I suppose) about four hundred Regulars in one Body, coming up the road, and marched toward the north part of the Common, back of the meeting-house of said Lexington; and as soon as said Regulars were against the east end of the meeting-house, the Commanding Officer said something, what I know not; but upon that the Regulars ran till they came within about eight or nine rods of about an Hundred of the Militia of Lexington, who were collected on said Common, at which time the Militia of Lexington dispersed; then the Officers made an huzza, and the private Soldiers succeeded them: Directly after this, an officer rode before the Regulars to the other side of the body, and hallooed after the Militia of said Lexington, and said, "Lay Down your Arms, Damn you, why Don't you lay Down your arms?" and that there was not a Gun fired till the Militia of Lexington were Dispersed; and further saith not."

Affidavit No. 3. Lexington, April 25, 1775:

"Simon Winship, of Lexington, in the County of Middlesex, and province of Massachusetts Bay, New England, being of lawful age, testifieth and saith, that on the Nineteenth of April Instant, about four o'Clock in the Morning, as he was passing the Publick Road in said Lexington, peaceably and unarmed, about two miles and an half distant from the meeting-House in said Lexington, he was met by a Body of the Kings regular Troops, and being stop'd by some Officers of said Troops, was Commanded to Dismount; upon asking why he must dismount, he was obliged by force to Quit his Horse, and ordered to march in the midst of the Body, and being Examined whether he had been Warning the Minute Men, he answered No, but had been out, and was then returning to his fathers. Said Winship further testifies, that he marched with said Troops, until he came within about half-a-Quarter of a Mile of said meeting-House, where an Officer commanded the Troops to halt, and then to prime and load: this being done, the said Troops marched on till they came within a few Rods of Captain Parkers Company, who were partly collected on the place of parade, when said Winship observed an Officer at the head of said Troops, flourishing his Sword, and with a Loud Voice, giving the word fire, fire, which was instantly followed by a Discharge of Arms from said regular Troops, and said Winship is positive, and in the most solemn manner declares, that there was no Discharge of arms on either side, till the word fire was given, by the said Officer as above."

Affidavit No. 4. Lexington, April 25, 1775:

"I, John Parker, of lawful Age, and Commander of the Militia in Lexington, do testify and declare, that on the 19th Instant in the Morning, about one of the Clock, being informed that there were a Number of Regular Officers, riding up and down the Road, stopping and insulting People as they passed the Road; and also was informed that a Number of Regular Troops were on their March from Boston in order to take the Province Stores at Concord, ordered our Militia to meet on the Common in said Lexington to consult what to do, and concluded not to be discovered, nor meddle or make with said Regular Troops (if they should approach) unless they should insult or molest us; and, upon their sudden Approach, I immediately ordered our Militia to disperse, and not to fire:--Immediately said Troops made their appearance and rushed furiously, fired upon, and killed eight of our Party without receiving any Provocation therefor from us."

Affidavit No. 5. Lexington, April 24, 1775:

"I, John Robins, being of lawful Age, do Testifye and say, that on the Nineteenth Instant, the Company under the Command of Captain John Parker, being drawn up (sometime before sun Rise) on the Green or Common, and I being in the front Rank, there suddenly appear'd a

Number of the Kings Troops, about a Thousand, as I thought, at the distance of about 60 or 70 yards from us Huzzaing, and on a quick pace towards us, with three Officers in their front on Horse Back, and on full Gallop towards us, the foremost of which cryed, throw down your Arms ye Villains, ye Rebels! Upon which said Company Dispersing, the foremost of the three Officers order'd their Men, saying, fire, by God, fire! At which Moment we received a very heavy and close fire from them, at which Instant, being wounded, I fell, and several of our men were shot Dead by me. Captain Parker's men I believe had not then fired a Gun, and further the Deponent saith not."

Affidavit No. 20. Medford, April 25, 1775:

"I, Edward T. Gould, of his Majesty's own Regiment of Foot, being of lawful Age, do testify and declare, that on the Evening of the 18th. Instant, under the Orders of General Gage, I embarked with the Light infantry and Grenadiers of the Line, commanded by Colonel Smith, and landed on the Marshes of Cambridge, from whence we proceeded to Lexington; On our arrival at that place, we saw a Body of provincial Troops armed, to the Number of about sixty or seventy Men; on our Approach, they dispersed, and soon after firing began, but which party fired first, I cannot exactly say, as our Troops rush'd on shouting, and huzzaing, previous to the firing, which was continued by our Troops, so long as any of the provincials were to be seen. From thence we marched to Concord. On a Hill near the Entrance of the Town, we saw another Body of provincials assembled; the light Infantry Companies were ordered up the Hill to disperse them; on our approach, they retreated towards Concord; the Grenadiers continued the Road under the Hill towards the Town. Six Companies of light Infantry were ordered down to take possession of the Bridge, which the provincials retreated over; the Company I commanded was one: three Companies of the above Detachment went forwards about Two Miles; in the mean Time, the provincial Troops returned, to the number of about three or four hundred: We drew up on the Concord side [of] the Bridge, the provincials came down upon us, upon which we engaged and gave the first Fire; This was the first Engagement after the one at Lexington; a continued firing from both parties lasted thro' the whole Day; I myself was wounded at the Attack of the Bridge, and am now treated with the greatest Humanity, and taken all possible Care of by the provincials at Medford."

Sylvanus Wood's Affidavit in 1826 was sworn before a Justice of the Peace and later published in 1858:

"I, Sylvanus Wood, of Woburn, in the county of Middlesex, and commonwealth of Massachusetts, aged seventy-four years, do testify and say, that on the morning of the 19th of April, 1775, I was an inhabitant of Woburn, living with Deacon Obadiah Kendall; that about an hour before the break of day on said morning, I heard the Lexington bell ring, and fearing there was difficulty there, I immediately arose, took my gun, and, with Robert Douglass, went in haste to Lexington, which was about three miles distant."

"When I arrived there, I inquired of Captain Parker, the commander of the Lexington Company, what was the news. Parker told me he did not know what to believe, for a man had come up about half an hour before, and informed him that the British troops were not on the road. But while we were talking, a messenger came up and told the captain that the British troops were within half a mile. Parker immediately turned to his drummer, William Diman, and ordered him to beat to arms, which was done. Captain Parker then asked me if I would parade with his company. I told him I would. Parker then asked me if the young man with me would parade. I spoke to Douglass, and he said he would follow the captain and me"

"By this time many of the company had gathered around the captain at the hearing of the drum, where we stood, which was about half way between the meeting-house and Buckman's tavern. Parker says to his men, "Every man of you, who is equipped, follow me; and those of you who are not equipped, go into the meeting-house and furnish yourselves from the magazine, and immediately join the company." Parker led those of us who were equipped to the north end of Lexington Common, near the Bedford road, and formed us in single file. I was stationed about in the centre of the company. While we were standing, I left my place, and went from one end of the company to the other, and counted every man who was paraded, and the whole number was thirty-eight, and no more."

"Just as I had finished, and got back to my place, I perceived the British troops had arrived on the spot between the meeting-house and Buckman's, near where Captain Parker stood when he first led off his men. The British troops immediately wheeled so as to cut off those who had gone into the meeting-house. The British troops approached us rapidly in platoons, with a general officer on horseback at their head. The officer came up to within about two rods of the centre of the company, where I stood, the first platoon being about three rods distant. They there halted. The officer then swung his sword, and said, "Lay down your arms, you damned rebels, or you are all dead men—Fire!" Some guns were fired by the British at us from the first platoon, but no person was killed or hurt, being probably charged only with powder."

"Just at this time, Captain Parker ordered every man to take care of himself. The company immediately dispersed; and while the company was dispersing and leaping over the wall, the second platoon of the British fired, and killed some of our men. There was not a gun fired by any of Captain Parker's company, within my knowledge. I was so situated that I must have known it, had any thing of the kind taken place before a total dispersion of our company. I have been intimately acquainted with the inhabitants of Lexington, and particularly with those of Captain Parker's company, and, with one exception, I have never heard any of them say or pretend that there was any firing at the British from Parker's company, or any individual in it, until within a year or two. One member of the company told me, many years since, that, after Parker's company had dispersed, and he was at some distance, he gave them 'the guts of his gun...'"

Sylvanus Wood, stated in his pension application (W19657), "I was then established at my trade two miles east of Lexington meetinghouse, on west border of Woburn, and on the nineteenth morn of April 1775, Robert Douglass and myself heard Lexington bell about one hour before day. We concluded that trouble was near. We waited for no man but hastened and joined Captain Parker's company at the breaking of the day. Douglass and myself stood together in the center of said company when the enemy first fired. The English soon were on their march for Concord. I helped carry six dead into the meetinghouse and then set out after the enemy and had not an armed man to go with me, but before I arrived at Concord I see one of the grenadiers standing sentinel. I cocked my piece and run up to him, seized his gun with my left hand. He surrendered his armor, one gun and bayonet, a large cutlash [cutlass] and brass fender, one box over the shoulder with twenty-two rounds, one box round the waist with eighteen rounds. This was the first prisoner that was known to be taken that day."

****

5:30 a.m. April 19, 1775

The British: Lieutenant Colonel Smith sends an express to General Gage to inform him as to what happened in Lexington. The Colonel tells his officers for the first time that Concord is their mission, and they are to destroy the supplies there. The march to Concord begins, and they will reach their destination before eight o'clock. The morale of the British troops is high due to their one-sided victory in Lexington.

The Americans: Many of Captain Parker's Company begin to return to the Green after the British march away. They make prisoners of six regulars who had wandered from the main body of troops for the purpose of plunder. They had entered a house for refreshments and were left behind. The prisoners are disarmed and later sent to Chelmsford.

After the troops pass toward Concord, Mrs. Hancock and Dorothy Quincy receive a letter from John Hancock stating where he and Samuel Adams are. He advises them to leave in the carriage and bring the fine salmon with them. The ladies leave and join them, but before they can eat the salmon, a man comes in yelling that the British soldiers are coming. So they leave without the food and travel to Amos Wyman's house in Billerica, where they eat cold salt pork and potatoes from a wooden tray. The alarm that the British soldiers are coming proves to be false.

Meanwhile, at Concord two companies of the Lincoln militia have arrived, followed by the minutemen from Acton. Soon to arrive are the minutemen from Groton and Bedford. Reuben Brown, who was present for the engagement at Lexington, rides in and tells the men that there was firing on the Lexington Common. Reuben tells Major John Buttrick of Concord, "I didn't wait to see whether bullets were being fired or just gunpowder." Emotions among the Americans are beginning to rise.

6:30 a.m. April 19, 1775

The British troops march through the part of Lincoln that is sparsely populated. They are unaware that most of the men in that town are in Concord waiting for them. The people of the town are well aware that the British are passing through. About 150 men from Concord are marching down the road and see in the distance the British heading their way. The Americans realize that the numbers are against them, so they turn around and quickly return to Concord.

Years later Amos Barrett wrote about the encounter with the British troops outside of Concord, "We marched down about a mile or a mile half and we see them acomming we halted and stay till they got within about 100 Rods [about 550 yards] then we was ordered to the about face and march before them with our Drums and fifes agoing and also the British we had grand musick."

Bureau of Engraving and Printing engraved vignette from the Battle of Lexington, based on a Darley drawing. The vignette appears on the left obverse of the $20 National Bank Note. Engraving by Luigi (Louis) Delnoce. (c. 1902).

PART IV

THE BATTLE OF CONCORD

"Let us stand our ground; if we die, let us die here."

----Rev. William Emerson, just before the Battle of Concord.

7:30 a.m. Wednesday April 19, 1775

Back in Boston: By this time General Gage receives the express from Lieutenant Colonel Smith that the British and Americans fired upon each other at Lexington.

In Concord:

The Americans: The minutemen arrive back at Concord with the British several hundred yards behind them. The leader of the Americans is Colonel James Barrett, 65 years old, and a veteran of the French and Indian War. He does not want the role of leader, because he feels he is too old. The men insist that he lead them, and he finally accepts under protest.

He addresses his men and reminds them of the danger to which they are exposed. He cautions them to be careful, not expose themselves needlessly, but be cool and firm. He tells them not to fire unless the British fire first. The Americans leave the town and occupy the ridge on the north side of the road. William Emerson later reported, "We formed into two Battalions, & waited the Arrival of the Enemy."

The British: There is no longer a need for secrecy for the movements of the British, as they march toward Concord beaming with great confidence. The soldiers want to finish the mission and get back to Boston, because by the time they get back they will have been without sleep for nearly twenty-four hours. They would have marched a total of thirty-two miles during this time.

The British march into town in two columns. One column is on the main road, and the other is north of the road on the ridge where the Americans are waiting. Before they search for military stores, they need to secure the two main bridges into town. The north and south bridges are the only approaches to the town from the west and northeast, because the water is unusually high this time of the year.

British entering Concord, engraving by Amos Doolittle.

As the British force march into town and take possession of the town square, Lieutenant Colonel Smith sees several hundred minutemen forming along the ridge to the north of the square. He quickly orders the light infantry out as flankers to clear the ridge. As the infantry goes up the ridge, the Americans pull back to another ridge without firing a shot. The Americans are now about half a mile north of the center of town and can observe all the British movements. They are nearly opposite the North Bridge that crosses the Concord River.

British forces are divided:

Lieutenant Colonel Smith and Major Pitcairn ride up the west end of the ridge vacated by the rebels and look through spyglasses at the surrounding countryside. They notice, "vast numbers assembling in many parts." Standing near them is the town's liberty pole with some type of flag on it. Smith orders the infantry to cut the pole down. [Later they will burn it.]

Smith orders six companies of light infantry to proceed to the North Bridge. He knows that the main task will be to hold this bridge. At the same time he dispatches Captain Munday Pole with a company of light infantry to hold the South Bridge and destroy any military stores found. Later minutemen from Sudbury are stopped about half a mile from the South Bridge by a messenger, Stephen Barrett, son of the American Colonel. The men are informed that the South Bridge is taken and is guarded by the British. The Americans must now march around to the North Bridge.

Smith orders his men to start searching the town for military stores. Ensign De Bernicre acts as a guide to the troops as to where they are found. De Bernicre visited the town on March 20, 1775 as a spy for General Gates, and he recorded the locations of military stores. At this time there are few people in the town, because they are either with the minutemen or somewhere outside of town hiding.

8:00 a.m. Wednesday April 19, 1775

The Americans: The Americans notice at once the six companies marching toward the North Bridge, and the officers begin to confer about what to do. Some want to withdraw until their strength is equal to the British, while some want to make a stand now. Rev. William Emerson is clear about his choice, "Let us stand our ground; if we die, let us die here." The consensus is to withdraw and wait for reinforcements. Colonel Barrett orders his men to retreat across the North Bridge. By the time they are out of musket range the British have taken command of the bridge.

Colonel Barrett takes the men about a mile north of town on Punkatasset Hill, which is a summit of about 200 feet. From there they can easily observe the British. This is the perfect location; they can see what is going on, and they can still be joined by the minutemen men that are coming from other towns

The British at North Bridge: At the bridge the British divide into two groups. Three companies under Captain Walter Laurie, who is relatively inexperienced, remain to guard the bridge. Laurie dispatches one company to the bridge, one company to a nearby hill, and the third company to another hill a quarter of a mile away.

One of the companies at the bridge marches to the Elisha Jones House nearby and surrounds the well in front of the house. The soldiers drink the cool water from the well, not knowing that inside the house just feet away in the cellar of the house are stores of fifty-five barrels of beef and nearly 1,700 pounds of salt fish.

According to tradition Elisha Jones was at home to protect the provisions in his cellar. After an exchange of fire at the North Bridge, Jones was supposed to have looked out the window at the gunfire. A British regular was said to have fired at Jones and struck the side of the house. The bullet hole is still there and the house became known as the "Bullet-Hole House." A Historical Structure Report by the National Park Service in 2007 could not prove or disprove this legend.

"The Bullet Hole"…fact or fiction? Library of Congress.

The second group of British troops consist of four companies under Captain Lawrence Parsons, who begins to march to Colonel Barrett's farm about two miles away. Intelligence gathered by the spy Ensign De Bernicre indicates there is military equipment stored there. According to the spy they will find gunpowder, weapons, and two cannons. Fortunately, most of the stores earlier had been concealed in a field. Barrett's sons had tilled the fields and buried some of the arms in the furrows of the field. Musket balls were taken to the attic and placed in barrels and then covered with feathers.

At the Barrett house the British soldiers ransack the house and demand food from Mrs. Barrett. She prepares food and drink for them which they pay for. At first she refuses payment and says it was her Christian duty to feed her enemies. They insist and throw the money in her lap. She accepts the money saying, "This is the price of blood." Captain Parsons will march back to the North Bridge empty-handed of rebel supplies.

The Barrett House, National Park Service

Meanwhile, back at the North Bridge Captain Walter Laurie is becoming increasing alarmed, because he sees more and more militiamen arriving. Men from Bedford, Chelmsford, Acton and Littleton have begun to arrive. The Captain sends a request to Lt. Colonel Smith for reinforcements. Colonel Smith sends another company to reinforce the troops guarding the bridge.

Destruction in the town: Major Pitcairn takes some soldiers to search the Wright Tavern owned by Ephraim Jones. Besides owning the tavern he is also the town jailer, and the jail is connected to the tavern. The British find the door to the tavern locked so they break it down. Pitcairn is the first to enter, where he encounters Jones. The tavern keeper knocks the officer to his knees with one punch. Jones in return is knocked down and secured by the soldiers. Pitcairn demands to know where the cannon is concealed. Jones refuses to say anything, so Pitcairn puts a pistol to his head.

Jones gives in and takes the British out to the prison yard where he shows them three iron twenty-four pounders mounted and ready for service. The cannons are left in plain sight, because they are too big to be hidden. The soldiers destroy the carriages and knock the trunnions off the guns. Pitcairn then sits down and orders breakfast, and soon the room is filled with British soldiers. While Smith is sitting at his table eating and drinking, he stirs sweetener in his drink and some spills over the side and onto the table. Smith compares the spill to the way Yankee blood will spill by nightfall.

Some of the soldiers go upstairs to open and search the rooms in the tavern. In one room they find a young servant girl, Hannah Barnes, blocking the door. She says the room and the chest inside are hers and for them to go away. The soldiers obey her command. Inside her room in the chest is the money of the Provincial treasury.

Wright's Tavern, built in 1747. National Park Service.

Some of the soldiers find a considerable quantity of flour stored in the malt-house. They roll the barrels down, break them in pieces, and then they scatter the flour in the street. At a gristmill nearby, a number of barrels are found which they throw into the mill-pond.

The British also abuse several people, which includes both men and women. One old man, Deacon Thomas Barrett the brother of the Colonel, stands in front of his house to protect it. He complains against their actions, so they threaten to kill him as a rebel. He tells them not to bother for he is old and will soon die. They reply, "Well, old daddy, you may go in peace." Inside of old man Barrett's house is a gun factory run by his son Samuel.

Martha Moulton of Concord said in a statement February 4, 1776, "Wherein I dwell, was beset with an army of regulars, who, in a hostile manner, entered the town, and drawed up in form before the door of the house where I live; and then they continued on the green, feeding their horses within five feet of the door; and about fifty or sixty of them was in and out of the house, calling for water and what they wanted."

The soldiers find several cannons which they spike. After looking further they find cannon balls, and they throw them into the mill-pond. [Later the townspeople were able to recover them]. The soldiers set fire to the courthouse, which also threatens other nearby houses and buildings.

On February 4, 1776 Martha Moulton petitioned for a pension to the General Court of Massachusetts and she stated,

> "When all on a sudden they had set fire to the great gun carriages just by the house, and while they were in flames your petitioner saw smoke arise out of the Town House higher than the ridge of the house. Then your petitioner did put her life, as it were, in her hand, and ventured to beg of the officers to send some of their men to put out the fire; but they took no notice, only sneered. Your petitioner, seeing the Town House on fire, and must in a few minutes be past recovery, did yet venture to expostulate with the officers just by her, as she stood with a pail of water in her hand, begging of them to send, etc. When they only said, 'O, mother, we won't do you any harm! Don't be concerned, mother,' and such like talk. The house still burning, and knowing that all the row of four or five houses, as well as the school house, was in certain danger, your petitioner (not knowing but she might provoke them by her insufficient pleading) yet ventured to put as much strength to her arguments as an unfortunate widow could think of; and so your petitioner can safely say that, under Divine Providence, she was an instrument in saving the Court House, and how many more is not certain, from being consumed, with a great deal of valuable furniture, and at great risk of her life. At last, by one pail of water after another, they sent and did extinguish the fire"

The committee in Concord aware of what she had done voted to pay her three pounds for successfully preventing the army from burning the down the courthouse and other structures.

At the house of Amos Woods the British begin searching inside. One room is locked, and Mrs. Wood tells the British officer that it contains frightened women. The officer, being a gallant gentleman tells his men not to enter the room. Inside the room is military equipment.

As the morning wears on the men become more concerned for food than military supplies. The men are not thrilled about eating army food consisting of terrible tasting salt pork. The home cooked food of the colonists is much more desirable. They don't seem to mind that with the food comes lectures from the townspeople about their behavior and the behavior of their government.

While the town is being searched by the British, it has not gone unnoticed by the Americans. The Americans look down from the surrounding hills at the British troops on the North Bridge and see the smoke of homes and businesses being burned in town. By now they have four times the number of men that the British have at the North Bridge. Even though the British have another 500 men in town the Americans know they can attack the bridge and fall back if needed. The officers begin to hold counsel to discuss what to do.

9:00 a.m. Wednesday April 19, 1775

Back in Boston: Earl Hugh Percy finally gets his delayed orders from Lieutenant Smith to leave Boston with a relief party. The order was issued hours earlier, but due to confusion Percy gets the orders late. A full Brigade of about 1,000 men and two pieces of artillery begin to leave Boston.

Along the way they march to the tune of "Yankee Doodle" which will taunt the Americans. Some of the patriots later said, "The British went out playing Yankee Doodle, and came back dancing it."

Deacon Ephraim Cutter used to tell his grandchildren how, when he was a boy of eight years old, he heard the footsteps of the soldiers marching as one man, and "saw the burnished arms and bright bayonets glittering in the sunlight, looking like a flowing river."

At Concord: The Americans look down at the troops on the bridge and in town they can see smoke rising into the air. They believe that their homes are being burned. Angered by the perceived burning of their homes they are ready, as Major Buttrick and Captain Davis say, "To march into the middle of the town for its defence, or die in the attempt."

Amos Baker thought to be "the sole survivor of the men who were present at the North Bridge at Concord," stated just months before his death in 1850,

> "When we were going to march down to the bridge, it was mentioned between Major Buttrick, and Capt. Isaac Davis, that the minute men had better be put in front, because they were the only men that had bayonets, and it was not certain whether the British would fire, or whether they would charge bayonets without firing. I do not remember which of them said it, but they both agreed to it; and Captain Davis's company of minute men [from Acton] was then brought up on the right. Then they saw the smoke of the town house, and, I think, Major Buttrick said "Will you stand here and let them burn the town down?""

The colonials at this time have over 400 men and there are about ninety-six British troops facing them at the bridge. Barrett gives the order to march but not to fire unless fired upon. Lieutenant Colonel John Robinson of Westford and Major John Buttrick of Concord lead the troops. The group includes three companies from Concord, the militia of Acton, Bedford, Lincoln, and a group of volunteers. A pair of fifers and drummers play "The White Cockade" as the minutemen march out.

Captain Laurie orders the British companies that are guarding the bridge to pull back across it. He has several men try to pull up the loose planks on the bridge to slow down the colonial advance. Major Buttrick sees what the British are doing and yells at the men to stop. The British soldiers stop pulling up the planks, not because the American yelled at them, but because they are less than 50 yards from them.

Seeing that he is in a precarious situation, Captain Laurie sends a desperate message back to Lieutenant Colonel Smith asking for reinforcements. Colonel Smith responds by organizing two companies to be sent in relief. Unfortunately he decides to lead them, but being a very large man and never in a hurry, he does not come close to arriving in time to do any good.

The inexperienced Captain Laurie then makes a poor tactical decision. He orders his men to form positions for "street firing." They line up in columns of four and the men in the first couple of ranks fire. After firing they break to the right and left, and then go to the rear to reload. The next group moves up, fires, and the process repeats itself. This is a good maneuver if you are fighting in a narrow street, but it's not in an area with an open path behind a bridge.

Lieutenant Sutherland is at the rear of the British guard, sees the tactical blunder, and orders flankers to be sent out from the column. Very few men obey him, which is either due to the noise or not being familiar with him giving commands to them.

9:30 a.m. Wednesday April 19, 1775

Shots fired at the bridge:

As the Americans approach the bridge a shot rings out and lands in the river, which is seen by Solomon Smith. [According to Captain Laurie's report to his commander after the fight, it was probably from a panicked, exhausted British soldier.] Immediately after the first shot two regulars fire, and their shots also splash in the river. Then before Captain Laurie can stop them a volley is fired by the troops in the front column.

Two of the Acton minutemen, Private Abner Hosmer and Captain Isaac Davis, who are at the head of the line marching to the bridge, are hit and killed instantly. Rev. Dr. Ripley later recalls, "Four more men were wounded. Major Buttrick then yelled to the militia, 'Fire, for God's sake, fellow soldiers, fire!'"

At this point the lines are separated by the Concord River and the bridge. They are only fifty yards apart. The few front rows of colonists, bound by the road and blocked from forming a line of fire, manage to fire over each other's heads and shoulders at the regulars massed across the bridge. Four of the eight British officers and sergeants, who are leading from the front of their troops, are wounded by the volley of musket fire. Soon at least three privates are killed or mortally wounded, and nine more are wounded. The firing on each side lasts but a minute or two.

The Battle of Concord Bridge, painting by Alonzo Chapell (1828-1887)

In an affidavit given on April 22, 1850 by Amos Baker who is the last survivor of the men present at the North Bridge states, "Before the fighting began, when we were on the hill, James Nichols of Lincoln, who was an Englishman, and a droll fellow, and a fine singer, said 'If any of you will hold my gun, I will go down and talk to them.' Some of them held his gun, and he went down alone to the British soldiers at the bridge, and talked to them some time. Then he came back and took his gun, and said he was going home, and went off before the fighting. Afterwards he deserted to the British."

Further research by this author revealed that James Nichols did not desert to the British, rather he served for several months in the Continental Army. He did desert once from the army, but later rejoined it.

Amos also states, "Joshua Brooks, of Lincoln, was at the bridge and was struck with a ball that cut through his hat, and drew blood on his forehead, and it looked as if it was cut with a knife; and we concluded they were firing jackknives. When we had fired at the bridge and killed the British, Noah Parkhurst, who was my right hand man, said, 'Now the war has begun and no one knows when it will end.'"

Many years later Amos Baker summed up the activities of the day when he said, "I verily believe that I felt better that day, take it all the day through, than if I had staid at home."

The regulars feel themselves trapped. They are greatly outnumbered, tired, most probably have little or no combat experience, their leadership has made poor decisions, and they probably did not expect to be shot at. So the men break, begin to pull back, and leave their wounded to take care of themselves. When they near the town they run into the slow moving reinforcements under Lieutenant Colonel Smith.

Colonel James Barrett gives a deposition before the Committee of the Provincial Congress on April 23, 1775, "I ordered them to march to the north bridge and pass the same, but not to fire on the king's troops, unless they were fired upon. We advanced near said bridge, when the said troops fired upon our militia and killed two men upon the sport, and wounded several others, which was the first firing of guns in the town of Concord. My detachment then returned the fire, which killed and wounded several of the king's troops."

Rather than pursue the British into Concord, Colonel Barrett moves his men back to the hilltop about 300 yards from the bridge. He sends Major Buttrick with some men to cross the bridge and to take a defensive position behind a stone wall. By moving his men back the Colonel gains a good defensive position. Also, up to now what had happened was a purely defensive action. If he advances to Concord it would be an attacking movement, which could be considered a declaration of war.

Meanwhile, four companies of British under Captain Parsons are at Colonel Barrett's farm looking for military stores. Before the firing at the bridge takes place, Parsons is marching his men back to the North Bridge. About a mile from the bridge they stop at Widow Brown's Tavern. The troops sit on the roadside having refreshments when the firing at the bridge begins. A young American boy, Charles Handley, later testifies that he hears the shots but the British appeared not to hear them. Handley said the soldiers remained on the side of the road drinking. The troops probably never imagined that the colonists would put up a fight.

Charles Handley's Deposition December 1, 1835, "I heard the guns, at the bridge, but the British did not appear to hear them. They marched on, very soon, but were in no haste. It was always said that they had no knowledge of the fight, till they passed the bridge, and saw the men that had been killed."

A few minutes after the fight at the bridge, a guard of British troops that are stationed near the place where they first entered the village, sees a rider approaching them. Riding toward them is Abel Prescott, who was sent that morning to take an express to the town of Sudbury. Prescott sees the guards, turns his horse around, and rides to the house of Mrs. Haywoood. She is in the house with her son-in-law, and they conceal Prescott in a dark place behind the chimney and a dry cask. Prescott hears the British in the house searching for him, but they cannot locate him. While these soldiers are at the house, they see a number of Americans running on the grounds towards a barn. The British fire at them, but the men get away.

General Percy's relief troops: After Percy leaves Boston they go south through Roxbury. Rumors of the skirmish at Lexington has reached the people there, and by the time the British pass through the minutemen begin to gather. They follow Percy's little army waiting for an opportune time to attack. Percy is delayed for a short time at Brighton Bridge, until the planks which were removed can be replaced.

Samuel Abbot Smith describes what happened, "Lord Percy's reinforcements had been delayed a little time at Brighton Bridge, the planks of which had been taken up by the direction of the Committee of safety. But, unfortunately, they were simple piled up on the Cambridge side, and it was the work of but a few moments to replace them sufficiently to allow the troops to pass."

Percy is mounted on a beautiful white horse leading his men through Roxbury, and he notices a young boy laughing as the British musicians play "Yankee Doodle." Percy asks the boy why he is laughing, and the boy replies, "To think how you will dance by-and-by to Chevy Chase." Percy feels uncomfortable the rest of the day because of the boy's reply.

["The Ballad of Chevy Chase" tells the story of a hunting party led by Percy on some hunting land or chase in the Cheviot Hills in England. The Scottish Earl of Douglas had forbidden this hunt and looked upon the excursion as an invasion of Scotland. A bloody battle was fought between the large hunting group and the Scots which resulted in the death of many.]

During the march Percy encounters an absent minded tutor, Isaac Smith, from Harvard College. Not sure which road to take, Percy asks the Harvard man. The man, oblivious to what is going on, points Percy in the right direction. Later, the poor man has to leave the area, because he is accused of aiding the enemy.

10:00 a.m. Wednesday April 19, 1775

The British in Concord:

Lieutenant Colonel Smith is concerned about the four companies commanded by Captain Parsons. The troops will not be protected when they march back to town. Smith notices some minutemen near the bridge kneeling behind a stone wall. Smith and several officers advance forward to get a closer look at the situation. Later one of the minutemen behind the wall notes, "If we had fired, I believe we could have killed almost every officer there was in the front, but we had no orders to fire and there wasn't a gun fired."

When Captain Parsons' men return from drinking at Widow Brown's Tavern, they see dead comrades on the side of the road near the bridge. One of the men they notice has been killed with a savage cut to the head with a hatchet.

As the fight at the bridge raged [according to tradition] a young boy, Ammi White, is chopping wood for a clergyman, and after the battle he goes with his axe in hand to the area. He finds a wounded British soldier, and as the man tries to rise the boy uses his axe to kill him. Later, the British publish that the Americans had scalped and cut the ears off their enemies. Both sides condemned the action and the young boy regretted it the rest of his life.

Mrs. Hulton, a Loyalist living in Boston, writes a letter in April of 1775, "two or three of their people (British) lying with agonies of death scalped and their noses cut off and eyes bored out..." Over time the number of men this happen too had grown to several. As late as 1841 a British historian says, "Several were scalped, or had their ears cut off, by the Americans."

10:00 a.m. Wednesday April 19, 1775

The British prepare to leave Concord:

Lieutenant Colonel Smith realizes that they are far from Boston and there may be dangers along the way, so he assembles his entire force in Concord village. He has many wounded soldiers and no way to transport them back. Smith confiscates carriages from locals Reuben Brown and John Beaton. He gets bedding from nearby houses. The carriage belonging to Reuben Brown is later left at West Cambridge and contains a wounded officer inside. The officer received kind attention from the Americans.

11:00 a.m. Wednesday April 19, 1775

Sometime before eleven-thirty Captain Parsons' men return to the center of Concord. They pass over the North Bridge without any interference from the Americans. The regulars are all in town, some are eating, and others are still searching for military supplies. The men under Captain Parsons begin telling the other troops about the mutilated soldier they had seen. A combination of fear and anger begins to rise in the troops. While the British delay leaving Concord it gives the Americans in outlying towns more time to reach the road back to Boston and prepare for the return trip of the British.

Noon Wednesday April 19, 1775

At Lexington: Captain Parker reorganizes his militiamen and are marching toward Concord. Marching with the men are several bandaged and wounded men. The Americans advance with a sense of determination and revenge, as they think of their dead friends in Lexington.

At Concord: The British are now fed, rested, and organized for their return to Boston. They leave Concord with flankers posted along the ridge on the north side of the road to Meriam's Corner. Little do they know they are about to run a seventeen mile long gauntlet, that will be known as "Battle Road."

PART V

BATTLE ROAD FROM CONCORD TO LEXINGTON

"Each American sought his own place and opportunity to attack and annoy the enemy from behind trees, rocks, fences, and buildings as seemed most convenient."

----Rev. Edmund Foster, on Battle Road.

Leaving Concord

12:30 p.m. Meriam Corner, Wednesday April 19, 1775

Americans: As the British are leaving Concord, the Americans that are at the North Bridge cross the "great field" located north of the town. The number of militia increases to over 1,100 with men coming from the towns of Billerica, Chelmsford, Reading, Woburn, Framingham, Sudbury, Westford, and Stow. For the first mile the British encounter no resistance.

At Meriam's Corner, about a mile from the center of Concord, the Reading companies are coming down the Bedford Road which runs into the Lexington Road. The Americans see the British flankers of nearly 100 soldiers rejoin the main British column. The Reading militia runs for the cover of the buildings and stone walls at the Meriam House and they wait for the British.

They arrive at Meriam's Corner about the same time as the retreating British. As the British cross a narrow bridge they fire a volley toward the Reading militia positioned around the Meriam House. The various militia companies move into the area, return fire killing two British privates, and wound several others.

Rev. Edmund Foster a private in the Reading Company gave this account,

"As soon as the British had gained the main road and passed a small bridge near the corner, they faced about suddenly and fired a volley of musketry upon us. They overshot; and on one to my knowledge was injured by the fire. The fire was immediately returned by the Americans, and two British soldiers fell dead at a little distance from each other in the road. Each American sought his own place and opportunity to attack and annoy the enemy from behind trees, rocks, fences, and buildings as seemed most convenient."

Rather than fight the traditional way, grouped together and facing the enemy, the Americans engage in a guerrilla type of warfare. They fight as individuals and hide behind objects along the side of the road. They fire and then melt away to reappear later down the road. They are not be able to defeat the British in a single battle, rather they slowly pick them off one by one. For the next 17 miles the British are sitting ducks. The British are bewildered and indignant, believing that this method of attack is dishonorable and murderous.

Reuben Eaton leaves the town of Reading and finds the British a little past Meriam's Corner so he hides behind a wall. As they approach he takes deliberate and careful aim and fires at them. He later says about the adventure, "O, it was glorious picking!"

One time Reuben is almost picked off himself. He stays at his firing place too long, and some British soldiers approach very close to him. Reuben starts to run, and the soldiers immediately fire at him. Reuben drops to the ground, although he is not hit. Thinking they killed him, the British soldiers move on. Reuben then jumps up and starts running again, and once more the musket balls come flying by him. Again he drops down on the ground like he is dead. After a minute or two Reuben jumps up and starts to run. The troops see him and fire, but he gets away unhurt. He does hear one soldier say, "See that Yankee; we have killed him twice, and look, he can run yet!"

British Lieutenant Colonel Smith tries to maintain his men in formation, except when he has to send out men in flanking movements. Many times these flankers catch the militiamen by surprise and kill some. Most of the forty-nine Americans killed this day are probably by flankers.

When leaving Meriam's Corner there is a wooded area around the road. Many of the Americans make for that woods and arrive just in time to meet the British. On the opposite side of the road is another group of Americans. The British now have to march between two groups of Americans firing at them. A quick battle takes place, and eight or more British soldiers are killed and many are wounded.

British relief troops: Around this time General Percy is marching through Menotomy. He has left Boston without extra ammunition for his men or for his two cannons. Percy believes that the supply wagons will slow him down. Each soldier has about 35 rounds, and there are only a few rounds of ammunition for the cannons. The supply wagons are more than 30 minutes behind him and without protection.

1:00 p.m. Brook's Hill, Wednesday April 19, 1775

A half mile east of the bridge at Meriam's Corner is Brook's or Hardy's Hill. Waiting for the British to arrive are minutemen from Sudbury and other towns. A total of 500 minutemen are located on the hill just south of the road. As the British approach, the Americans keep a steady fire on the British below them. Colonel Smith sends some flanking troops charging up the hill after the Americans. The Americans hold their ground and inflict significant causalities upon the attackers.

Smith withdraws his flankers from Brook's Hill, and the column continues on to another small bridge into Lincoln. There more militia companies intensify the attack on the retreating British from the north side of the road. Around this time men from Woburn arrive 180 strong, and the fighting becomes heavy. During the battle Sergeant Ford, who had fought in the French and Indian wars, kills five of the British soldiers.

1:30 a.m. Bloody Angle, Wednesday April 19, 1775

The British reach an area of the road, where the road rises, then curves sharply to the left, and goes through a little wooded area. [This sharp curve will become known as "Bloody Angle."] The British begin taking fire from behind them and to their left and right. A militia company from Woburn takes up a position on the south side of the road, militia from the engagement at Meriam's Corner attack from behind, and additional minutemen line the north side of the road. Immediately, eight British soldiers are killed and the retreat becomes a rout. The British troops begin to panic and start to flee in confusion.

Some of the minutemen get careless during the attack, and British flankers sent out from the main body kill three Americans including Captain Jonathan Wilson of Bedford. Another 500 yards down the road there is another sharp curve, and once again the British are caught in a crossfire. Passing through these two curves cost the British thirty killed or wounded. The British soldiers escape by breaking into a trot, which is a pace that the colonials cannot maintain through the woods and swampy terrain. The American forces now number in excess of 2,000 men of all ages.

In nearby Lincoln the women of the town know that their men are in this part of the fight, and that the men will pass this way down the road. So, the ladies turn out and prepare a lunch of hasty pudding and milk at the home of Leonard Hoar. "This," said Mrs. Farrar of Lincoln, "was hastily served on extemporized tables of barrels and boards by the roadside."

Up the road another half mile are three structures a few hundred feet apart. The tavern is owned by Ephraim Hartwell, the Hartwell house owned by Sergeant John Hartwell of the Lincoln minutemen, and there is the Captain William Smith house.

A British soldier is killed on the side of the road between the Hartwell house and the tavern. Another is wounded and left to die near the Smith house. Members of the town carry the wounded soldier into one of the homes and dress his wounds. The soldier dies several days later.

Mrs. Samuel Hartwell shows her compassion for the slain soldiers when she later writes. "I could not sleep that night, for I knew there were British soldiers lying dead by the roadside; and when, on the following morning, we were somewhat calmed and rested, we gave attention to the burial of those whom their comrades had failed to take away. The men hitched the oxen to the cart, and went down below the house, and gathered up the dead. As they returned with the team and the dead soldiers, my thoughts went out for the wives, parents, children away across the Atlantic, who would never see their loved ones."

During the fight a Lincoln minuteman William Thorning lays in one of the holes in a field and begins firing at the British. They discover his hiding place and return fire. William escapes by lying in another trench and waiting for the British to pass by. Minutes later William runs to a pasture and hides behind a large bolder and begins firing again, and this time he kills two British soldiers. The rock he hides by later becomes known as "Minute Man Bolder."

A few hundred yards down the road stands the home of Samuel Hastings. Samuel, not at home, is among the Americans chasing the British. One of the British soldiers leaves the ranks and enters the Hastings house for plunder, ignoring the danger that lurks all around him. As he leaves he stands in the doorway and is shot. He lays there until the family returns later in the afternoon.

They carry the soldier into the house and care for him the best they can, but the wound proves to be fatal. After the man dies they find some of their silver spoons in his pocket. The soldier is buried a short distance from the house.

General Percy's supply wagons:

Several miles behind Percy the supply wagons, consisting of two wagons guarded by fourteen men, are now entering Menotomy. They have had great difficulty ever since they left Boston. In Cambridge they had trouble crossing the Brighton Bridge, and later they are misled by false directions and become so far separated that they cannot receive any protection from Percy's men. Word has reached Menotomy that the unprotected supply wagons are approaching the town.

Waiting for the convoy of wagons is twelve old men called "exempts." They are exempt for serving in the militia because of their advanced age, but many are experienced fighters of the French and Indian Wars. The old men elect David Lampson to be their leader.

David Lampson, a free black man, told the following story to Colonel Thomas Russell, who told it to Samuel Abbot Smith who wrote about it in his book,

"Meanwhile an express was sent post-haste from Old Cambridge to Menotomy, bearing the information that these supplies were on the way. Several of our men met at once in Cooper's tavern, which stood on the present site of Whittemore's hotel, to form some plan for capturing them. They were of the exempts, or alarm list as it was called, all old men, for every young man was that day nearer the post of danger. There were Jason Belknap and Joe Belknap, James Budge, Israel Mead and Ammi Cutter, David Lampson, and others, in all twelve. Some of them had been soldiers in the French war, and age had not impaired their courage. They chose for their leader David Lampson, a mulatto, who had served in the war, a man of undoubted bravery and determination."

The twelve men take a position behind a wall of earth and stones, and they wait for the groups of wagons. According to Samuel Smith's book,

"The convoy soon made its appearance. As it came between them and the meeting house of the First Parish, Lampson ordered his men to rise and aim directly at the horses, and called out to them to surrender. No reply was made, but the drivers whipped up their teams. Lampson's men then fired, killing several of the horses, and, according to some accounts, killing two of the men and wounding others."

Once the firing begins, the drivers jump from their wagons and run to the bank of Spy Pond. They throw their guns into the pond and then continue to run along the banks of the pond, and soon they are met by an old woman named Mother Batherick.

As reported in Smith's book, "They surrendered themselves to Mother Batherick who was digging dandelions. She led them to the house of Capt. Ephraim Frost, where there was a party of our men, saying to her prisoners, as she gave them up. 'If you ever live to get back, you tell King George that an old woman took six of his grenadier's prisoner.'"

Once the wagons are captured, David Lampson has his men take the wagons down into a hollow and allows anyone to take what they want. A thirteen year old boy takes a soldier's pack and blanket, and he hurries off to his home. When his mother sees what the boy has she does not let him inside the house, fearing that it will draw upon themselves the vengeance of the British. The British dead are dragged to a field and secretly buried so not to draw the wrath of the British.

These old men have the honor of making the first capture of British provisions of the American Revolution. The following later makes the rounds in some of the British newspapers. "If one old Yankee woman can take six grenadiers, How many will be required to conquer America?"

2:00 p.m. Lexington, Wednesday April 19, 1775

As Percy's troops arrive in Lexington they can hear gunfire in the distance. Colonel Smith and his men approach the Lexington border; and are thankful to be leaving the heavy fighting of Lincoln behind. Instead, they march into fire from the 120 men waiting there. This ambush is set by Captain John Parker's Lexington militia, which includes some of the men bandaged up from the encounter at Lexington earlier in the day.

2:30 p.m. Fisk Hill, Wednesday April 19, 1775

Colonel Smith is attempting to rally his men on Fiske Hill, or at least restore some order to the retreat. At this point Lt. Colonel Smith is wounded in the thigh and knocked from his horse. Major John Pitcairn assumes effective command of the column and sends light infantry companies up the hill to clear the militia forces. The British officers place themselves in front and threaten every man with death if they leave the line.

The troops start to form when one of the musket volleys from the American soldiers causes Major Pitcairn's horse to bolt in fright, which throws Pitcairn to the ground and injures his arm. Now, both principal leaders of the expedition are injured or unhorsed, and their men are tired, thirsty, and exhausting their ammunition.

Edmund Foster was an eye-witness to Pitcairn's injury, "The enemy were then rising and passing over Fiske's Hill. An officer, mounted on an elegant horse, and with a drawn sword in his hand, was riding backwards and forwards, commanding and urging on the British troops. A number of Americans behind a pile of rails, raised their guns and fired with deadly effect. The officer fell, and the horse took fright, leaped the wall, and ran directly towards those who had killed his rider."

Pitcairn of course is not killed. The horse is captured by the Americans and later sold at auction. On the animal are Pitcairn's pistols which are carried for the remainder of the war by Israel Putnam. They will later be donated to the Lexington Historical society.

British casualties are mounting from these engagements and from persistent long-range fire from the militiamen, as a result some of the British surrender or they are captured. Other men begin to panic, and they break rank and run. According to one British officer, "we began to run rather than retreat in order. ... We attempted to stop the men and form them two deep, but to no purpose, the confusion increased rather than lessened…the officers got to the front and presented their bayonets, and told the men if they advanced they should die. Upon this, they began to form up under heavy fire."

Down the easterly slope of Fiske Hill is the farmhouse of Benjamin Fiske. This is where [told earlier in this book] James Hayward and a British soldier shoot each other at the same time, and James' father later finds his son and is able to talk to him before the boy dies.

Near the old poorhouse outside of Lexington the British are almost out of ammunition, and as they run they leave many of their wounded and dead behind. When Lexington Green comes into view the soldiers see the relief column of General Percy, and they know they are saved. The men, disregarding all orders, break and run for Lexington. If Lord Percy had not arrived at this time Colonel Smith and his men would have been wiped out.

Even in the heat of battle, acts of kindness and mercy are found. Edmund Foster gives aid to a wounded British soldier and two others that are wounded near the poorhouse. He takes them to safety at Buckman's Tavern in Lexington.

Caesar and John Ferrit, both Indians raised in an American family, arrive at a house near the Lexington meeting house as the retreating British enter Lexington. Both men fire their muskets at the British troops from the door of the house, and then they hide under the cellar stairs as the British search for them in the house.

General Percy forms his men in lines across the road on high ground, where they can see down the road about a mile. They see the fleeing mob of British soldiers chased by a large group of rebels. Percy orders his cannons to open fire at extreme range. The cannon fire causes very little damage, but help to disperse the Americans.

American Colonel Loammi Baldwin wrote in his diary, "The enemy marched very fast, and left many dead and wounded and a few tired. I proceeded on till coming between the meeting-house and Buckman's Tavern with a prisoner before me, when the cannon began to play, the balls flew near me, I judged not more than two yards off. I immediately retreated back the meeting-house, and had not been there ten seconds before a ball come through the meeting-house near my head. I retreated back towards the meadow, north of the meeting-house, and lay and heard the balls in the air and saw them strike the ground."

Rev. Joseph Thaxter, who would later be wounded at Bunker Hill, wrote in the U.S. Literary Gazette in 1825, "We pursued them and killed some; when they got to Lexington, they were so close pursued and fatigued, that they must have soon surrendered, had not Lord Percy met them with a large reinforcement and two field-pieces. They fired them, but the balls went high over our heads. But no cannon ever did more execution, such stories of their effects had been spread by the tories."

Some of the militia from Newton, under the command of Colonel Michael Jackson, try to flank Percy's men, but the General sends out flanking troops and stops them. These troops are some of their best marksmen and are under orders to shoot at any Americans that show themselves. Jackson's men join with some men from Watertown, and they stay on the British flank all the way back to East Cambridge.

Smith's men collapse with exhaustion once they reach the safety of Percy's lines. The British soldier and spy De Berniere describes the march to Lexington, "All the hills on each side of us were covered with rebels—there could not be less than 5,000; so that they kept the road always lined and a very hot fire on us without intermission, when we arrived within a mile of Lexington, our ammunition began to fail." Since the Americans keep up a steady fire from all sides, it is understandable why De Berniere thought that there were more than 5,000 minutemen attacking them.

PART VI

BATTLE ROAD FROM LEXINGTON TO BOSTON

"For my part, I never believe, I confess, that they would have attacked the Kings troops, or have had the perseverance I found in them yesterday."

----General Percy's report after he returned to Boston.

3:00 p.m. Lexington, Wednesday April 19, 1775

When Lieutenant Colonel Smith's men enter the safety of Lexington they are, as one man describes, "so much exhausted with fatigue, that they were obliged to lie down for rest on the ground, their tongues hanging out of their mouths, like those of dogs after a chase." His troops have been up since ten o'clock the evening before, they have marched over twenty-three miles, and for the last several hours they have been under constant fire. As General Percy writes the next day, "I had the happiness of saving them from inevitable destruction."

General Percy takes control of the combined British forces of about 1,500 men, and he orders the destruction of any structure that can be used as cover for the sniping Americans. Three houses and some buildings are then burned. Some of Percy's troops begin to wander around Lexington looting and burning some of the houses and businesses. Several of the Lexington residents later testify, "After burning Several Buildings the troops marched through the remaining part of town they Continued plundering the houses of many of their valuable Effect, Breaking windows, & Doors and all Kinds of Mischief they had time Accomplished till they passed the Town."

On the other hand, Percy later states in one of his letters, "His Majesty's Troops during the whole affair behaved with their usual intrepidity & spirit. Nor were they a little exasperated at the cruelty and barbarity of the Rebels, who scalped & cut off the ears of some of the wounded men who fell into their hands." There was no mention of burning and looting of homes.

The wounded British soldiers are taken to Munroe Tavern and treated. John Raymond an elderly and lame man is there checking on the tavern on behalf of its owner. He is ordered to serve the British soldiers drinks. When he sees a chance, he escapes out the back door and is shot and killed by the soldiers.

Marksmen from the militia manage to creep in close and keep up the firing. As minutemen run out of ammunition some return home. However many more continue to join the increasing ranks of the Americans.

3:30 p.m. The Retreat Resumes, Wednesday April 19, 1775

The British: As the British march east toward Menotomy four and a half miles away, General Percy puts out flankers to prevent the Americans from getting too close. The flankers also begin to pillage houses near the roadside.

Thanks to information from Colonel Smith and Pitcairn about how the Americans have been attacking the troops, Percy reorganizes his troops. He orders the rear guard to be rotated every mile to allow some of his troops to briefly rest. He wants his strongest troops on the sides and rear. He places Smith and his tired soldiers at the front of the column, where he expects little trouble. The wounded in the borrowed carriages are placed in the middle of the troops.

Percy later writes in his official report, "As it now began to grow pretty late and we had fifteen miles to retire, and only our thirty-six rounds, I ordered the Grenadiers and Light Infantry to move off first, and covered them with my Brigade, sending out very strong flanking parties."

Soon the flanking soldiers begin to loot and pillage houses near the roadside, without any interference from their officers. Some of them break into an old tavern where Mr. Cutler, a rich farmer, lives. The soldiers carry off what they can, leave the taps of the molasses and spirit casks open, destroy furniture, and set the house on fire. A faithful slave, who is watching from a safe distance, extinguishes the flames as soon as the soldiers leave.

Deacon Joseph Adams sees the soldiers and flees across the fields with the enemy in pursuit. They fire at him several times, and he runs into a barn, climbs up into the hayloft, and covers himself with hay. The soldiers come in, begin to search for him, and stick their bayonets here and there into the hay. Afraid to remain too long they leave, and Adams is able to escape.

As the troops pass one woman's home, she stands in her doorway firing at them. She is told to stop, but she continues to fire and yelling insults. The soldiers shoot her, and everyone in the house.

The march is a slow one, because Smith's tired and wounded soldiers have to be considered. Some of the men drop out of the ranks for good. One soldier, a German, is discovered by the roadside after Percy's men pass out of sight. The Americans treat him with kindness, and he later makes his home among them for many years.

The British orders of the day are very simple. If any American snipers are caught in a house or around it, kill them. If need be, burn the house. If there is a large scale assault by the Americans the cannons will be used. The troops do not stop, but continue the advance to Boston and safety.

The Americans: William Heath, one of the five generals appointed by the Provincial Congress to take charge of the Militia, arrives at Lexington with Dr. Joseph Warren. [Dr. Warren will later die in battle at the Battle of Bunker Hill.] Heath and Warren react to Percy's artillery and flankers by ordering the militiamen to avoid close formations that will attract cannon fire. Instead, they surround Percy's marching square with a moving ring of skirmishers at a distance to inflict maximum casualties at a minimum risk.

General William E. Heath, PD-US

Heath has the American commanders of several regiments circle around the British force and attack, as the British retreat down the road. He tells the men to take over any abandoned house on or near the road, and to convert it into a strong fort.

He has a company of men from Watertown to go to Cambridge, and he instructs them to again dismantle the bridge over which Percy had earlier passed. Then they are to barricade the bridgehead and make a stand there.

Once the British depart Lexington, people in the town turn their attention to the Americans that had died earlier on Lexington Green. They hold a simple service over them conducted by Rev. Jonas Clarke. They carry the dead to the churchyard and place them in one large grave. The people are afraid that the British will come back, take vengeance on them, and perhaps on the dead. The grave is dug in the remote part of the yard, and the fresh mound of dirt is hidden beneath branches cut from nearby trees.

Jonas Clarke Jr. later tells of the service, "Father, Mother, and me and the baby went to the Meeting House, there was the eight men that was killed, seven of them my Father's parishioners, one from Woburn, all in Boxes made of four large Boards. Nailed up and, after Pa had prayed, they were put into two horse carts and took into the grave yard where Father and some Neighbors had made a large trench, as near the Woods as possible and there we followed the bodies of those first slain, Father, Mother, I and the Baby, there I stood and there I saw them let down into the ground, it was a little rainey but we waited to see them covered up with the Clods and then for fear the British should find them, my Father thought some of the men had best Cut some pine or oak bows and spread them on their place of burial so that it looked like a heap of brush."

The total number of Americans in pursuit of Percy after he leaves Lexington is around 2,000 men. People from surrounding towns send wagons with food and ammunition to help the patriots.

4:30 p.m. Pierce's Hill, Wednesday April 19, 1775

All along the march the British are under fire from Americans, who will fire and then disappear. When the flanking troops have to move toward the road because of the terrain, then the Americans creep closer and fire. When the flanking soldiers move out away from the road, the Americans slip away out of reach.

After traveling about two and a half miles from Lexington, the British have to climb Pierce's Hill located on the west side of the town of Menotomy. About a half a mile farther the ground is again lowered at an area known as the "Foot of the Rocks". By this time there are over 2,000 militiamen in about thirty-five companies. This is a large amount of firepower to throw at the retreating British. Some of the day's bloodiest fighting is about to occur. Although no more than 400 or 500 minutemen are actually engaged at one time, the conflict is continuous.

It is at the "Foot of the Rocks" that Dr. Warren exposes himself to a British marksman. The bullet comes so close to the head of the doctor that it strikes a pin from his ear-lock. Some of the fighting becomes hand-to-hand. This is where Dr. Eliphalet Downer of Brookline hits an enemy soldier with the butt of his musket, and then when the soldier drops his musket the doctor finishes him off with the soldier's own bayonet.

Later during the day Dr. Downer sees a wounded British soldier lying in a barn. He asks the soldier if he would like for him to dress his wound. The soldier grabs his gun and says, "Damn yer, I'll dress yer wound for yer!" Before the soldier can shoot the doctor, another American shoots the soldier.

During the fighting General Percy has a button shot off his uniform. The firing becomes so intense that the General finally halts the column and brings the cannons up. Once they fire, stone walls are knocked down and holes and put in houses. This forces the Americans to scattered.

Cuff Whittemore is a slave and a member of the Memotomy militia. Captain Thomas of the militia relates this story,

"Cuff was on the hill with the Memotomy militia, of which Solomon Bowman was Lieutenant, and on the opening of the fight at that point, which was evidently near the house of Jason Russell of Arlington, the negro acted cowardly, and in his alarm turned to run down the hill. But the Lieutenant threatened to shoot him with a horse pistol, and pricked him in the leg with the point of the sword. This brought Cuff to his senses, and the negro "about facing" fought through the contest, as the colonel said, like a wounded elephant, making two cuss'd Britishers bite the dust." Cuff continues to serve in the revolution and gains his freedom after the war.

Battle Road, print by A.H. Ritchie. National Archives.

4:45 p.m. Menotomy, Wednesday April 19, 1775

As the British entered Menotomy and musket fire erupts from the first houses, Percy orders Lt. Col. Smith's troops to split into squads and attack every building with their bayonets. It was later reported, "The soldiers were…enraged at suffering from an unseen enemy."

Several British soldiers enter one house where there were two old men. One is a deacon of the church, who is bedridden, and the other not able to walk is sitting in his chair. Both men are stabbed and killed on the spot, as well as a child running out of the house.

The Russell house: Jason Russell age fifty-eight sends his wife and children away to safety and he stays to guard his house. A neighbor, Ammi Cutter, who had earlier helped to capture several British supply wagons, tries to get Russell to leave. Russell refuses saying, "An Englishman's house is his castle."

Some of the minutemen of Danvers, under Lieutenant Gideon Foster, station themselves around the Russell House and use bundles of shingles as a barrier. They soon find themselves nearly surrounded. Seven of the young men of Danvers are killed in the yard. One of the men killed is twenty-two year old Jotham Webb, who had been married only a few weeks. When the call came early that morning, Jotham put on his wedding clothes saying, "If I die, I will die in my best clothes." A poem is later written about the young man.

"A gallant hero, too, was Webb,

Nor deemed his nuptial suit too fine

In which to act a soldier's part

And pour his gifts at Freedom's shrine;

But donned his best, and kissed his bride,

And sped to make the sacrifice—

The wedding garb his glory shroud,

The fatal ball his pearl of price."

As the British close in, eight men run inside the house and downstairs to the cellar. Daniel Townsend and Timothy Munroe are standing beside the Russell house firing at British troops. Townsend had just fired and says, "There is another redcoat down." Munroe looking around realizes that they are completely hemmed in by the flank guard. The two men race inside the house and find that they are now trapped inside.

Jason Russell who was outside the house also runs to the front door to get inside. Unfortunately, Russell is lame and is hit by two bullets. As he lays in the doorway bleeding, the British soldiers bayonet him eleven times.

When the British enter the house Townsend jumps through a window but is shot dead outside by flankers. Later, when his body is found he has forty ball holes through his clothes. Munroe follows through the window and is shot in the leg. He rises to his feet and manages to escape with thirty-two ball holes in his hat and clothes. Even the metal buttons of his waistcoat are shot off. As he passes the last British soldier to fire he hears the man say, "Damn the Yankee, he is bullet proof, let him go."

Perhaps Munroe is able to escape because of a good deed earlier in the day. Munroe had come upon a wounded British soldier, who begged him to dress his wound. Munroe used his handkerchief to stop the flowing blood from the wound. To reward him for his kindness the soldier gave him a silver buckle from his clothes.

The eight Americans, who earlier ran downstairs into the cellar, stand waiting for any British soldier to dare to come down the stairs after them. One brave, or perhaps foolish soldier, does go down and is instantly shot. The rest of the British soldiers leave the house. The eight lucky men in the cellar are able to escape with their lives.

In the area Pastor Samuel Phillips Payson from Chelsea arrives with some of his men. Before the day began the Pastor was friendly to the Royal Government. After he had learned what had happen at Lexington he became a supporter of the patriot cause. Payson and his men attack a group of twelve British soldiers carrying supplies they had looted. The Americans kill one British soldier and capture the rest.

An account in the August 2, 1775 *Pennsylvania Journal* stated:

"The Rev. Mr. Payson, of Chelsea, in Massachusetts Bay, a mild, thoughtful, sensible man, at the head of a party of his own parish, attacked a party of regulars, killed some and took the rest prisoners. This gentleman has been hitherto on the side of government, but oppression having got to that pitch beyond which even a wise man cannot bear, he has taken up arms in defense of those rights, civil and religious, which cost their forefathers so dearly."

After the British leave the area, neighbors gather the dead Americans around the Russell house and place them side by side in a single room. When Mrs. Russell later comes home she finds her husband and eleven minutemen dead on the floor. She says that the blood in the room is almost ankle deep. One of the Russell family members later recalls, "Our house was a sad place that night."

Other women returning home that day also find blood on the floors of their homes from the hand-to-hand fighting. On down the road from the Russell house is the Adams house. It is punctured with bullets, and the dead and wounded are carried inside after the British march on.

When Mrs. Butterfield returns to her home she finds her best bed covered with blood and an English officer lying in it. Another bed contains a wounded American soldier. Mrs. Butterfield does everything she can to try and save the life of the British officer. Later when she was treating the officer a neighbor came in and called her a tory and threaten to kill the wounded officer. Mrs. Butterfield told the man, "Only a coward would want to kill a dying man." The American recovers, but the British officer dies after about a week.

Cooper's Tavern:

General Percy has lost control of his men, and the soldiers begin to commit atrocities to repay for the reported scalping at the North Bridge, for their own causalities, and because the minutemen will not stand and fight as soldiers should. Old men are bayonetted without mercy, and women and children are driven from their homes screaming into the fields as their homes are torched.

Several British officers are not happy by the plundering of their men. One later calls it shameful and writes, "some soldiers hardly thought of anything else, what was worse, they were encouraged by some officers."

The British troops continue to plunder houses all the way to Cooper's Tavern. While the fighting outside is going on, inside the tavern Jason Winship and Jabez Wyman are enjoying a drink at the tavern. Unfortunately for them, it is on the route of the British soldiers' fleeing to safety in Boston. So many houses along the road have concealed minutemen in them, and this tavern is no different to the British soldiers. The soldiers break into the tavern and murder the two men as they drink their ale. Benjamin and Rachael Cooper are behind the bar and escape to the cellar.

A month after the incident, Mrs. Cooper was interviewed and described the dramatic scene, "The King's regular troops under the command of General Gage, upon their return from blood and slaughter, which they had made at Lexington and Concord, fired more than one hundred bullets into the house where we dwell, through doors, and windows,…The two aged gentlemen [Winship and Wyman] were immediately most barbarously and inhumanly murdered by them, being stabbed through in many places, their heads mangled, skulls broke, and their brains out on the floor and walls of the house."

Down the road the British are about to encounter the oldest soldier they face that day. When the British first marched by in the morning, Samuel Whittemore got up from bed and watched them go by. That afternoon he is ready for their return trip.

Samuel is seventy-eight, according to some historians he may have been a few years older, and no stranger to soldiering. He fought in King George's War in 1745 as a member of the British Royal Dragoons. That afternoon Samuel is out working in the fields, when he hears gunfire as the returning British enter the town of Menotomy again.

Samuel, who is crippled, limps back to his house and gathers his weapons. His family is stunned, as they watch him load his musket and both of his dueling pistols. He puts powder and ball in his old worn military knapsack from the war of 1745. He then straps his French made saber around his large waist and starts walking toward the door. [People used to ask Samuel, "How did you get this French Saber?" He would reply, "The man I got it from died suddenly."]

His family begs him not to go, and one of the family members tells him that the British will take him. Samuel tells them that the British will find it hard work to do so. He then says "I'm going to fight some British regulars."

He walks up to [what is today Massachusetts Street] a secluded position behind a stone wall across the street from the church. Other patriots in the town are firing at the British as they march through town. Samuel waits patiently until about a dozen troops are marching near him. He fires his musket, and then he fires his two pistols killing one of the British and wounding two others. Samuel does not have time to reload his weapons, so he draws his old saber and begins swinging it and cursing the Redcoats who had now surrounded him. They quickly overpower the old man and shoot him in the face, tearing half his cheek away, and knock him down. Samuel tries to rise to continue the fight, but the British club him with their musket butts and bayonet him numerous times. Believing the old man is dead they continue their march.

After the British have left, the townspeople come out to retrieve the body of Samuel and are astonished that he is still alive. They use a door as a stretcher and carry the bloody body to Cooper's Tavern, which is serving as a hospital for the wounded. Doctor Cotton Tufts from Medford takes a look at Samuel and says there is no use even dressing the wounds, because he is going to die. At the insistence of some of Samuel's friends the doctor dresses the wounds and cleans the body.

The next day in Boston an informant overhears some British soldiers talking about the fight on the road from Concord to Boston. One of the soldiers remarks, "We killed an old devil there in Menotomy." Another soldier adds, "But we paid most dear for it—lost three of our men, the last died this morning."

Samuel had the last laugh, because he survived and lived another eighteen years! The people account for his longevity by saying that "he bled like an ox" from his wounds and through the new blood formed he gets a new lease on life. It takes several weeks before Samuel, due to the serious head wound, begins to recognize family members. One asks him if he regrets his actions. Samuel says, "No. I should do just so again."

When the British finally leave Menotomy they have at least forty men killed, which is over half of their entire losses for the day. The Americans have at least twenty-two militiamen killed that afternoon. The fighting is still not over.

PART VII

BACK TO BOSTON

"The country is all in arms and we are absolutely invested with many thousand men, some of them so daring as to come very near our outpost on the only entrance into town by land. They have cut off all supplies of provisions from the country."

----British officer the morning of April 20, 1775.

5:30 p.m. The Last Few Miles, Wednesday April 19, 1775

Cambridge:

As the British march into Cambridge the fighting grows intense. Fresh militiamen arrive, and Percy once again has to use his artillery to keep the Americans at a manageable distance. The Americans begin to occupy Prospect Hill, until Percy moves his cannons to the front and disperses them. The Militia now number nearly 4,000.

Watson's corner:

A mile beyond the Menotomy River a small group of Americans wait behind a pile of empty casks in the yard of Jacob Watson, a blacksmith. The British flank guard comes up unobserved and completely surprises the Americans, and during the day they kill the highest ranking officer on either side, Major Isaac Gardner of the Brookline Militia. He is pierced twelve times by bullets and bayonet wounds, and he becomes the first Harvard graduate to die in the Revolution.

Three other Americans are also killed here; John Hicks, Moses Richardson, and William Marcy. Hicks' wife sends their fourteen year old son to look for her husband. The boy finds his father lying dead by the side of the road. The remains of Hicks and Richardson are taken by a cart to a little churchyard a mile away, and they are placed in one grave without coffins or shrouds. One of the sons of Moses Richardson stands over the grave and realizes that the dirt will fall directly on his father's face. He jumps into the grave and arranges the cape of his father's coat, so that his face will be protected from the dirt.

Near the same place, William Marcy, a man "of feeble intellect" sits on a wall watching and enjoying the military show. His friendly shouting and clapping results in a British soldier shooting him dead.

While this skirmish is taking place, Dr. William Aspinwall, the son-in-law of Major Isaac Gardner, feels sure that the British will not proceed down that road toward the Cambridge Bridge, but instead he believes that Percy will take the road to Charlestown. [It was a good move on Percy's part because the Americans have removed many of the planks on the bridge as they were ordered.]

Dr. Aspinwall sees a detachment of Americans, under Captain Gridley, and he hastens to tell the Captain what he believes Percy will do. Captain Gridley pays no heed to his suggestions. However, when Dr. Aspinwall sees he is right and the British are actually taking the road leading to Charlestown, he leaps upon a wall and cries out: "There they go, boys! Whoever wants a chance to do some good, follow me!" About half of the little company instantly follows the doctor and pursues the enemy till dusk, into the neighborhood of Charlestown. The doctor is blind in one eye and when firing at the British has to aim from the left shoulder. As awkward as it is, he is still an excellent shot.

6:00 p.m. Wednesday April 19, 1775

Somerville:

In Somerville the British pause at a small pond for the troops to get water, and some of them even jump in for a refreshing dip. As the British pass Prospect Hill they can see safety in sight. The people of Boston are on the hill watching the fight and flight of the British.

A little farther up the road some of the troops enter the Shed home for plunder. One of the soldiers remains too long, so when his comrades leave he doesn't realize that he is alone. Americans come up the road, see him inside, and shoot him through the window.

Several yards down the road sixty-six year old James Miller and a companion wait for the British. As the British approach, the two men fire several times. They are soon discovered by the British and the companion says, "Come, Miller, we've got to go." Miller replies, "I'm too old to run." Miller remains and is shot thirteen times by the soldiers.

The British have a policy of shooting into houses, where residents who might be potential snipers, are seen. Edward Barber, fourteen years old, falls victim to this policy, when he runs to look out the window as the troops pass. He is spotted by a soldier, and he is killed with one shot in front of his brothers and sisters who then run screaming into the street.

Children die on the British side as well. During the retreat Joshua Simonds captures two soldiers, and one is just a small boy who plays the flute. The boy's coat is buttoned all the way to his chin, which conceals a musket ball wound. A farm family takes the boy in to nurse him, but he dies several days later.

A large militia force, under Colonel Timothy Pickering, arrives and could have cut Percy's route to the safety of Charlestown, but the Colonel halts his men on nearby Winter Hill. Later some critics believed that he chose not to advance because of sympathy for the British.

Timothy Pickering

After 6:30 p.m. Wednesday April 19, 1775

Charlestown:

When firing is heard in Cambridge people begin to flee toward Charlestown Neck, where they meet the retreating British troops. This causes them to again flee in panic back to their homes. Rumors begin to circulate of the British killing women and children in the streets. There is another report that the slaves are intending to rise up and finish what the British have done to the women and children.

On Prospect Hill some women gather at a home, when they see Ishmael, a Negro slave belonging to Mr. Cutler, approach the house. Thinking their time has come, one of the women asks the slave, "Are you going to kill us, Ishmael?" "Lord-a-massy, no ma'am!" says the surprised Slave. "Is my missis here?"

Even with all the panic and fear, there can be found romance. John Tufts has arrived from Somerville to take part in the day's events. He happens to meet a young woman, Elizabeth Perry, wandering very frightened in the fields. John, twenty years old, has never seen the young woman and offers her his protection, which she is most happy to accept. [They later married and had thirteen children.]

All during the day in Charlestown there is excitement. Dr. Warren rides through town in the morning spreading news of the bloodshed in Lexington. Some men grab their muskets and leave to join the fight. Schools and shops are closed, and many townspeople begin to panic and flee. They gradually return when they learn that there is no danger to them.

When the British arrive in Charlestown, American General Heath orders his men to stop the pursuit. The last American soldier killed is probably a young black man who is wounded and killed near the houses close to the Charlestown Neck. This probably is the slave, Caesar Augustus, owned by Mr. Tileston. Once they reach Charlestown the British has flankers take the high ground, and this places them under the protection of the guns of the HMS *Somerset*.

As the sun sets at seven o'clock it is followed by a thunderstorm that soaks the tired men. The main body of troops establish camp and occupy Bunker Hill. Reinforcements are sent out by General Gage and stationed in various parts of town, and the wounded are taken to local hospitals.

Cannons have won the day for the British. Had it not been for the cannons, the British army could have been completely defeated. It kept the Americans at a safe distance and from forming in large numbers. The British learn that the Americans were not a bunch of rabble cowards to be taken lightly. The Americans learn that the British were not invincible, and that much could be achieved when they were united.

On May 24 the *Pennsylvania Journal* stated,

"The British officers and soldiers have done ample justice to the bravery and conduct of the Massachusetts militia—they say that no troops ever behaved with more resolution. A soldier who had been in the action, being congratulated by a fellow soldier on his safe return to Boston, declared, 'That the militia had fought like bears, and that he would as soon attempt to storm hell, as to fight them a second time.'"

****

By April 20, 1775 the colonial forces grow as militias from New Hampshire, Rhode Island, and Connecticut arrive outside of Boston. New Hampshire troops, in response to the Lexington alarm, assemble at Medford where the field officers meet. They advise the men to enlist in the service of the Massachusetts's colony. Connecticut votes to raise more than 6,000 men. Rhode Island votes to raise 1,500 men under the command of Brigadier General Nathanael Greene.

Soon Boston is surrounded by a huge militia army from New England numbering over 15,000 men. They form a siege line extending from Chelsea, around the peninsulas of Boston and

Charlestown, to Roxbury, which effectively surrounds Boston on three sides. The Siege of Boston has begun. On June 17, 1775 some of these men fight at Bunker Hill and on July 3, 1775 George Washington assumes command of the army.

On April 20, 1775, the day after his reinforcements meet up with British Lt. Colonel Smith's troops in Lexington for the long difficult march back to Boston, British General Percy writes the following,

"During the whole affair, the rebels attacked us in a very scattered irregular manner, but with perseverance and resolution, nor did they ever dare to form into any regular body. Indeed they knew too well what was proper, to do so. Whoever looks upon them as an irregular mob, will find himself very much mistaken. They have men amongst them who know very well what they are about, having been employed as rangers against the Indians and Canadians, and this country being much covered with wood, and hilly, is very advantageous for their method of fighting. For my part, I never believed, I confess, that they would have attacked the king's troops, or have had the perseverance I found in them yesterday."

PART VIII

LOSSES

"It is well that war is so terrible, or we should grow too fond of it."

----Robert E. Lee

Names of known American men killed

LEXINGTON:

Jonas Parker: He is shot, and while on his knees trying to reload he is bayoneted.

Samuel Hadley: He is killed on Lexington Green.

Caleb Harrington: He is killed on Lexington Green.

Robert Munroe: He is killed on Lexington Green.

Isaac Muzzy: He is killed on Lexington Green.

John Brown: He is killed on Lexington Green.

Jonathon Harrington, Jr.: He is shot and manages to crawl back to his home, and dies on his own doorstep in the arms of his wife.

Jedediah Munroe: He is wounded at Lexington in the morning and killed there in the afternoon during the British retreat.

John Raymond: He is killed at Lexington during the British retreat. He is forced to serve the British at Munroe Tavern, and when he tries to escape he is shot.

Nathaniel Wyman: He is from Billerica but is a member of the Lexington militia. He is killed at "Bloody Angle" on Battle Road.

CAMBRIDGE and MENOTOMY:

William Marcy: He is a "simple-minded youth" who is killed while thinking he is watching a parade.

Moses Richardson: He is caught by surprise by British flankers at Watson's Corner in Cambridge.

John Hicks: He is caught by surprise by British flankers at Watson's Corner in Cambridge.

Jason Russell: He is shot and bayoneted in the doorway of his home in Cambridge.

Jabez Wyman: He is drinking in Cooper's Tavern when the British enter and kill him.

Jason Winship: He is drinking in Cooper's Tavern when the British enter and kill him.

NEEDHAM: At Menotomy the retreating British send infantry men to flank the main body of troops, and they came up and shot these five men from behind:

John Bacon
Elisha Mills
Amos Mills
Nathaniel Chamberlain
Jonathan Parker

SUDBURY:

Josiah Haynes: He is killed at the age of seventy-nine as the British retreat through Lexington.
Asahel Reed: He is killed as the British retreat through Lexington.

WOBURN:

Daniel Thompson: He and the rest of the men from Woburn were on either side of Bedford Road in Lincoln just a few miles from Concord. When the British arrived Daniel took cover behind a barn and began firing. A British soldier snuck up behind him and shot him in the back.
Asahel Porter: Asahel Porter returned home from Boston earlier that morning and was taken prisoner by the British troops. He attempted to escape during the Battle of Lexington when he was shot.

BEDFORD:

Captain Jonathan Wilson: He is shot and then bayoneted at Merriam's' Corner on Battle Road.

MEDFORD:

Henry Putnam: He is sixty-five years old, is exempt from military duty due to his age, but he fights anyway. He is killed at Menotomy.

William Polly: He is shot by the British while he is riding on his horse a distance from the main road in Menotomy. He dies six days later at the age of eighteen.

CHARLESTOWN:

James Miller: He is killed at his house while firing at the British. At the age of sixty-five he says he is too old to run from them.

Edward Barber: He is just fourteen and is killed looking out the widow of his home as the British are marching by.

WATERTOWN:

Joseph Coolidge: He participated in the Boston Tea Party. He is working in the field one day when he hears of the shooting at Lexington. He drops his plough, gathers his musket, powder, and never returns home. He dies on Battle Road.

DEDHAM:

Elias Haven: He is killed in Menotomy near the Russell house.

BROOKLINE:

Isaac Gardner: He is killed by British flankers at Watson's Corner. His body has twelve bullet and bayonet wounds in it.

DANVERS: All of the men die at, or near the Russell house in Menotomy.

Henry Jacobs

Samuel Cook

Ebenezer Goldthwait

George Southwick

Benjamin Daland, Jr.

Jotham Webb

Perely Putnam

SALEM:

Benjamin Pierce: He is killed in the yard of the Russell house in Menotomy.

BEVERLY:

Reuben Kennison: He is killed late in the day in the yard of the Russell house in Menotomy.

ACTON:

Isaac Davis: He has a premonition of his death when he tells his wife good-bye. He dies, shot through the heart at the North Bridge in Concord.

Abner Hosmer: He is a twenty-one year old drummer killed at the North Bridge in Concord.

James Hayward: He and a British soldier fire at the same time. The British soldier is killed, and James later dies at the side of Battle Road west of Lexington at Fiske farm.

LYNN:

Abednego Ramsdell: He is killed at the Russell house in Menotomy.
Daniel Townsend: He is killed when he jumps out of the window at the Russell house in Menotomy.
William Flint: He is killed at the Russell house in Menotomy.
Thomas Hadley: He is killed at the Russell house in Menotomy.

Total Americans: 49 killed 39 wounded, and 5 reported as missing.

British losses by some accounts are 73 killed, 174 wounded, and 26 missing. Of the 73 killed, 18 are commissioned officers.

PART IX

Propaganda of Lexington and Concord

"The first casualty when war comes is truth,"
----Hiram Johnson U.S. Senator

The British Version of the Battle of Lexington and Concord

The British version of the Battle of Lexington and Concord is presented in this broadside. It accuses the Americans of scalping and mutilation of one British officer while he is still alive. This report clearly puts the blame of what happens in Lexington on the Americans.

****

A Circumstantial Account
Of an Attack that happened on the 19th of April 1775, on his
Majesty's Troops

By a Number of the People of the Province of MASSACHUSETTS-BAY.

"On Tuesday the 18th of April, about half past 10 at Night, Lieutenant Colonel Smith of the 10th Regiment, embarked from the Common at Boston, with the Grenadiers and Light Infantry of the Troops there, and landed on the opposite side, from whence he began his march towards Concord, where he was ordered to destroy a Magazine of Military Stores, deposited there for the Use of an Army to be assembled, in Order to act against his Majesty, and his Government. The Colonel called his Officers together, and gave Orders, that the troops should not fire, unless fired upon; and after marching a few Miles, detached six Companies of Light Infantry, under the Command of Major Pitcarin, to take possession of two bridges on the other side of Concord: Soon after they heard many Signal Guns, and the ringing of Alarm Bells repeatedly, which convinced them that the Country was rising to oppose them, and that it was a preconceived scheme to oppose the King's Troops, wherever there should be a favorable Opportunity for it. About 3 o'clock the next morning, the Troops being advanced within two Miles of Lexington, Intelligence was received that about Five Hundred Men in Arms, were there, and determined to oppose the King's Troops; and on Major Pitcarin's galloping up to the Head of the advanced Companies, two officers informed him that a Man advanced from those that were assembled had presented his Musquet and attempted to shoot them, but the Piece flashed in the Pan: On this the Major gave directions to the troops to move forward, but on no Account to fire, not even to attempt it without orders. When they arrived at the End of the Village, they observed about 200 armed Men, drawn up on a Green, and when the Troops came within a Hundred Yards of them, they began to file off toward some Stone Walls, on their right flank: The Light Infantry observing this, ran after them; the Major instantly called to the Soldiers not to fire, but to surround and disarm them; some of them who had jumped over a Wall, then fired four or five Shot at the Troops, wounded a Man of the 10th Regiment, and the Major's Horse in two Places, and at the same Time several Shots were fired from a Meeting-House on the left: Upon this, without any Order or Regularity, the Light Infantry began a scattered Fire, and killed several of the Country People; but were silenced as soon as the Authority of their Officers could make them."

"After this, Colonel Smith marched up with the Remainder of the Detachment, and the whole Body proceeded to Concord, where they arrived about 9 o'clock, without any Thing further happening; but vast numbers of armed People were seen assembling on all the Heights: while Colonel Smith with the Grenadiers, and Part of the Light Infantry remained at Concord, to search for Cannon, &cc. there: he detached Captain Parsons with six Light Companies to secure a Bridge at some Distance from Concord, and to proceed thence to certain Houses, where it was supposed there was Cannon, and Ammunition; Captain Parsons in pursuance of these Orders, posted three companies at the Bridge, and on some Heights near it, under the command of Captain Laurie of the 43d Regiment and with the remainder went and destroyed some cannon wheels, powder and ball; the people still continued increasing on the heights, and in about an hour after, a large body of them began to move toward the bridge, the light companies of the 4th and 10th then descended, and joined Captain Laurie, the people continued to advance in great numbers and fired upon the King's troops, killed three men, wounded four officers, one Sergeant, and four private men, upon which (after returning the fire) Captain Laurie and his officers thought it prudent to retreat toward the main body at Concord and were soon joined by two companies of grenadiers. When Captain Parsons returned with the three companies over the bridge, they observed three solders on the ground, one of them scalped, his head much mangled and his ears cut off, though not quite dead, a sight which struck the soldiers with horror. Captain Parsons marched on and joined the main body, who were only waiting for his coming up, to march back to Boston. Colonel Smith had executed his orders without opposition, by destroying all the military stores he could find. Both the Colonel and Major Pitcarin having taken all possible pains to convince the inhabitants that no injury was intended them and that if they opened their doors when required to search for the said stores, not the slightest mischief should be done, neither had any of the people the least occasion to complain, but they were sulky and one of them even struck Major Pitcarin. Except upon Captain Laurie at the bridge, no hostilities happened from the affair at Lexington until the troops began their march back. As soon as the troops had got out of the town of Concord, they received a heavy fire on all sides, from walls, fences, houses, trees, barns, &c, which continued without intermission till they met the first brigade with two field pieces near Lexington ordered out under the command of Lord Percy to support them (advice having been received about 7 o'clock next morning that signals had been made and expresses gone out to alarm the country and that the people were rising to attack the troops under Colonel Smith). Upon the firing of the field pieces, the people's fire was for a while silenced, but as they still continued to increase greatly in numbers, they fired again as before from all places where they could find cover upon the whole body and continued doing so for the space of fifteen miles. Notwithstanding their numbers, they did not attack openly during the whole day, but kept under cover on all occasions. The troops were very much fatigued, the greater part of them having been kept under arms all night and made a march of upwards of forty miles before they arrived at Charlestown, from whence they were ferryed over to Boston."

"The troops had above Fifty killed, and many more wounded: Reports are various about the Loss sustained by the Country People, some make it very considerable, others not so much."

"Thus this unfortunate Affair has happened through the Ruthless and Imprudence of a few people who began Firing on the Troops at Lexington."

****

A British officer who took part in the skirmish at Concord described the event in a letter to the Massachusetts Governor shortly after the battle:

Lieut. Col. Smith to Governor Gage Boston, April 22, 1775.

"Sir, In obedience to your Excellency's commands, I marched on the evening of the 18th inst. with the corps of grenadiers and light infantry for Concord, to execute your Excellency's orders with respect to destroying all ammunition, artillery, tents, &c., collected there, which was effected, having knocked off the trunnions of three pieces of iron ordnance, some new gun carriages, a great number of carriage wheels burnt, a considerable quantity of flour, some gunpowder and musket balls, with other small articles thrown into the river. Notwithstanding we marched with the utmost expedition and secrecy, we found the country had intelligence or strong suspicion of our coming, and fired many signal guns, and rung the alarm bells repeatedly; and were informed, when at Concord, that some cannon had been taken out of the town that day, that others, with some stores, had been carried three days before. . . ."

"I think it proper to observe, that when I had got some miles on the march from Boston, I detached six light infantry companies to march with all expedition to seize the two bridges on different roads beyond Concord. On these companies' arrival at Lexington, I understand, from the report of Major Pitcairn, who was with them, and from many officers, that they found on a green close to the road a body of the country people drawn up in military order, with arms and accoutrements, and, as appeared after, loaded; and that they had posted some men in a dwelling and Meeting-house."

"Our troops advanced towards them, without any intention of injuring them, further than to inquire the reason of their being thus assembled, and, if not satisfactory, to have secured their arms; but they in confusion went off, principally to the left, only one of them fired before he went off, and three or four more jumped over a wall and fired from behind it among the soldiers; on which the troops returned it, and killed several of them."

"They likewise fired on the soldiers from the Meeting and dwelling-house. We had one man wounded, and Major Pitcairn's horse shot in two places. Rather earlier than this, on the road, a country man from behind a wall had snapped his piece at Lieutenants Adair and Sutherland, but it flashed and did not go off. After this we saw some in the woods, but marched on to Concord without anything further happening."

"At Concord we found very few inhabitants in the town; those we met with both Major Pitcairn and myself took all possible pains to convince that we meant them no injury, and that if they opened their doors when required to search for military stores, not the slightest mischief would be done. We had opportunities of convincing them of our good intentions, but they were sulky; and one of them even struck Major Pitcairn."

"While at Concord we saw vast numbers assembling in many parts; at one of the bridges they marched down, with a very considerable body, on the light infantry posted there. On their coming pretty near, one of our men fired on them, which they returned; on which an action ensued, and some few were killed and wounded. In this affair, it appears that after the bridge was quitted, they scalped and otherwise ill-treated one or two of the men who were either killed or severely wounded, being seen by a party that marched by soon after."

"On our leaving Concord to return to Boston, they began to fire on us from behind the walls, ditches, trees, etc., which, as we marched, increased to a very great degree, and continued without the intermission of five minutes altogether, for, I believe, upwards of eighteen miles; so that I can't think but it must have been a preconcerted scheme in them, to attack the King's troops the first favorable opportunity that offered, otherwise, I think they could not, in so short a time as from our marching out, have raised such a numerous body, and for so great a space of ground. Notwithstanding the enemy's numbers, they did not make one gallant effort during so long an action, though our men were so very much fatigued, but kept under cover."

****

The following is from a letter written by a British soldier about the events of April 19th. The letter comes from Boston on April 28, 1775.

"I am well, all but a wound I received through the leg by a ball from one of the Bostonians. At the time I wrote you from Quebec, I had the strongest assurance of going home, but the laying the tax on New England people caused us to be ordered for Boston, where we remained in peace with the inhabitants, till, on the night of the 18th of April, twenty-one companies of grenadiers and light infantry were ordered into the country, about eighteen miles; where, between four and five o'clock in the morning, we met an incredible number of the people of the country in arms against us. Col. Smith, of the 10th regiment, ordered us to rush on them with our bayonets fixed; at which time, some of the peasants fired upon us, and our men returning the fire, the engagement began; they did not fight us like a regular army, only like savages, behind trees and stone walls, and out of the woods and fields. The engagement began between four and five in the morning, and lasted till eight at night. I cannot be sure when you will get another letter from me, as this extensive continent is all in arms against us. These people are very numerous, and full as bad as the Indians for scalping and cutting the dead men's ears and noses off, and those they get alive, that are wounded and cannot get off the ground."

****

The following letter is written by Lord Hugh Percy to the Duke of Northumberland on April 20, 1775,

"I was ordered out yesterday morning to cover the retreat of the Grenadiers and Lgt Infy, who had been sent uopn an exped into the country. I had with my Brigade 2 pieces of cannon. We met them at a Town about 15 miles off, sharply attacked & surrounded by the Rebels, having fired away almost all their from inevitable destruction, & arrived with them at Chastown, opposite Boston ab' 8 o'clock last night, not, however, without the loss of a great many, having been under an incessant fire for 15 miles."

"The Rebels, however, have suffered much more than the King's Troops. I have not rec even the least scratch, so I beg you will not be uneasy on my account. There can now surely be no doubt of their being in open rebellion, for they fired first upon the King's Troops, as they were marching quietly along."

****

Of Anne Hulton's published letters the most frequently studied have been those written during 1767-1776, collected in *Letters of a Loyalist Lady* (1927). In this letter to her friend

Elizabeth Lightbody back in England, Anne Hulton described the actions of the Minutemen, whom she called the *banditti*, during the Battle of Lexington and Concord, April 19, 1775:

"On the 18th instant at 11 at night, about 800 grenadiers and light infantry were ferried across the bay to Cambridge; from whence they marched to Concord, about 20 miles. The congress had been lately assembled at that place, and it was imagined that the general had intelligence of a magazine being formed there and that they were going to destroy it."

"The people in the country (who are all furnished with arms and have what they call minute companies in every town ready to march on any alarm) had a signal, it's supposed, by a light from one of the steeples in town, upon the troops embarking. The alarm spread through the country so that before daybreak the people in general were in arms and on their march to Concord."

"About daybreak a number of the people appeared before the troops near Lexington. They were called to, to disperse, when they fired on the troops and ran off. Upon which the light infantry pursued them and brought down about fifteen of them. The troops went on to Concord and executed the business they were sent on, and on their return found two or three of their people lying in the agonies of death, scalped and their noses and ears cut off and eyes bored out, which exasperated the soldiers exceedingly, a prodigious number of people now occupying the hills, woods, and stone walls along the road."

"The light troops drove some parties from the hills, but all the road being enclosed with stone walls served as a cover to the rebels, from whence they fired on the troops still running off whenever they had fired, but still supplied by fresh numbers who came from many parts of the country. In this manner were the troops harassed in their return for seven [or] eight miles. They were almost exhausted and had expended near the whole of their ammunition when, to their great joy, they were relieved by a brigade of troops under the command of Lord Percy with two pieces of artillery."

"The troops now combated with fresh ardor and marched in their return with undaunted countenances, receiving sheets of fire all the way for many miles, yet having no visible enemy to combat with, for they never would face them in an open field, but always skulked and fired from behind walls and trees, and out of windows of houses, but this cost them dear for the soldiers entered those dwellings and put all the men to death."

"Lord Percy has gained great honor by his conduct through this day of severe service; he was exposed to the hottest of the fire and animated the troops with great coolness and spirit. Several officers are wounded and about 100 soldiers. The killed amount to near so; as to the enemy we can have no exact account, but it is said there was about ten times the number of them engaged and that near 2000 of them have fallen."

"The troops returned to Charlestown about sunset after having some of them marched near fifty miles, and being engaged from daybreak in action, without respite or refreshment, and about ten in the evening they were brought back to Boston. The next day the country poured down its thousands, and at this time from the entrance of Boston Neck at Roxbury round by Cambridge to Charlestown is surrounded by at least 20,000 men, who are raising batteries on three or four different hills."

"We are now cut off from all communication with the country, and many people must soon perish with famine in this place. Some families have laid in store of provisions against a siege. We are threatened, that whilst the outlines are attacked, with a rising of the inhabitants within, and fire and sword, a dreadful prospect before us, and you know how many and how dear are the objects of our care. The Lord preserve us all and grant us an happy issue out of these troubles."

****

The American Version of the Battle of Lexington and Concord

This is the American version about what happens at Lexington and Concord. The American version states that there was between 30 and 40 people at the meeting house in Lexington. The British version had the number at 200. Both versions differ on who fired first.

From E. Russell's *Salem* Gazette, or *Newbury* and *Marblehead* Advertiser, published on Friday, April 21, 1775,

"On Tuesday evening the eighteenth instant, a body of soldiers under the command of Lieutenant-Colonel *Smith*, to the amount of about eight hundred men, embarked from Barton's-Point in *Boston* about eleven o'clock, crossed Charles river, landed at Phip's farm in Cambridge and marched immediately to Lexington, near twelve miles from Boston. At sunrise, they observing between thirty and forty inhabitants exercising near the meeting house, the commanding officer ordered them to lay down their arms and disperse, which not being directly complied with, he *"damned them for a pack of rebels,"* ordered his men to fire upon them and killed eight men on the spot, besides wounding several more. The army then proceeded to Concord, drew up on the parade near the meeting house, during which time the inhabitants from the neighboring towns collected and took possession of the adjacent hills, about eleven o'clock firing began on both sides which lasted nearly an hour, when the regular troops began to retreat, the provincials closely pursuing them to a bridge at a small distance which the rebels took up as they passed; they then renewed the fire and some were slain on both sides. But the regulars still retreated and the provincials pursued them down to Lexington where the regulars, about three o'clock in the afternoon, met with a reinforcement of about twelve hundred men under the command of Earl Percy, with two brass field pieces, they then renewed the attack upon the provincials, but soon thought proper to retreat towards [*missing*] provincials pursued them into Charlestown, where they arrived about [*missing*] immediately an advantageous [*missing*] Bunker's-Hill, about a mile [*missing*] the provincials now discontinued the pursuit. The loss on either side [*missing*] not been able to ascertain, but it is about one hundred regulars killed and fifty wounded, among which were [*missing*] officers. Two officers and a number of soldiers were taken prisoner. On the side of the province, we hear that thirty-five were slain and several wounded. The above is as particular an account of the engagement as can at this time be [*missing*] in the present confused state of the province."

****

The following article is from the April 28, 1825 *Eastern Argus.* It describes the battle at Concord. Elijah Sanderson told his story for the 50th anniversary of the battle,

"I, ELIJAH SANDERSON, of Salem, in the country of Essex, cabinet-maker, aged seventy-three years, on oath depose as follows:

"I went to the tavern. The citizens were coming and going; Some went down to find whether the British were coming; some came back; and said there was no truth in it. I went to sleep in my chair by the fire. In short time after, the drum bent, and I ran out to the common, where the militia were parading. The captain ordered them to fall in. I then fell in. I was all in the utmost haste. The British troops were then coming on in full sight. I had no musket: having sent it home, the night previous, by my brother, before I started for Concord-and, reflecting I was of no use, I stepped out again from the company, about two rods, and was gazing at the British, coming on in full career. Several mounted British officers were forward—I think, five—The commander rode up, with his pistol in his hand, on a canter, the others following, to about eight or ten rods from the company perhaps nearer, and ordered them to disperse. The words he used were harsh. I cannot remember them exactly. He then said 'Fire and he fired his own pistol, and the other officers soon fired, and with that the main body came up and fired, but did not take sight. They loaded again as soon as possible. All was smoke when the foot fired. I heard no particular orders after what the commander first said. I looked and seeing nobody fall ought to be sure they couldn't be firing balls and I did not move off. After our militia had dispersed, I saw them firing at one man, (Solomon Brown,) who was stationed behind a wall, I saw the wall smoke with the bullets hitting it. I they knew they were firing balls."

"After the affair was over, he told me he fired into a solid column of them, and then retreated. He was in the cow-yard. The wall saved him. He legged it just about the time I went away. In a minute or two after, the British music struck up, and their troops paraded and marched right off for Concord."

"I went home after my gun—found it was gone. My brother had it. I returned to the meeting house, and saw to the dead. I saw blood where the column of the British had stood when Solomon Brown fired at them. This was several rods from where any of our militia stood, and I then supposed, as well as the rest of us, that that was the blood of the British. I assisted in carrying some of the dead into the meeting house."

"Some days before the battle, I was conversing with Jonas Parker, who was killed, and heard him express his determination never to run from before the British troops."

"In the afternoon I saw the reinforcement come up under Lord Percy. I then had no musket; and retired to Easterbrook's Hill, whence I saw the reinforcement meet the troops retreating from Concord. When they met, they halted some time. After this, they set fire to Deacon Boring's barn—then to his house—then to widow Mullikan's house—then to the shop of Nathanial Mullikan, a watch and clock maker—and to the house and shop of Joshua Bond. All these were near the place where the reinforcements took refreshments. They hove fire into several other buildings. It was extinguished after their retreat."

"During the day the women and children, had been so scattered and dispersed, that most of them were out of the way when the reinforcements arrived. I now own the musket, which I then owned and which my brother had that day, and told me be fired at the British with it."   Elijah Sanderson.

****

Part of Affidavit No. 18 at Worcester, April 26, 1775,

"Hannah Bradish, of that part of Cambridge, called Menotomy, and daughter of timothy Paine, of Worcester, in the county of Worcester, esq. of lawful age, testifies and says, that five o'clock on Wednesday last, afternoon, being in her bed-chamber, with her infant child, about eight days old, she was surprised by the firing of the king's troops and our people, on their return from Concord. She being weak and unable to go out of her house, in order to secure herself and family, they all retired into the kitchen, in the back part of the house. She soon found the house surrounded with the king's troops; that upon observation made, at least seventy bullets were shot into the front part of the house; several bullets lodged in the kitchen where she was, and one passed through an easy chair she had just gone from. The door of the front part of the house was broken open; she did not see any soldiers in the house, but supposed, by the noise, they were in the front. After the troops had gone off, she missed the following things, which, she verily believes, were taken out of the house by the king's troops, viz: one rich brocade gown, called a negligée, one lutestring gown, one white quilt, one pair of brocade shoes, three shifts, eight white aprons, three caps, one case of ivory knives and forks, and several other small articles.about"

****

Pastor Joseph Thaxter was at the Battle of Concord on April 19, 1775. He and Pastor William Emerson were under the command of Major Buttrick. Joseph, who had been preaching at

Westford, was in the front line armed with a brace of pistols. On November 30, 1824 Joseph Thaxter wrote in a letter the following account of the Battles of Concord,

"I was an eyewitness to the following facts. The people of Westford and Acton, some few of Concord, were the first who faced the British at Concord Bridge. The British had placed about ninety men as a guard at the North Bridge; we had then no certain information that any had been killed at Lexington, we saw the British making destruction in the town of Concord; it was proposed to advance to the bridge; on this Colonel Robinson, of Westford, together with Major Buttrick, took the lead; strict orders were given not to fire, unless the British fired first; when they advanced about halfway on the causeway the British fired one gun, a second, a third, and then the whole body; they killed Colonel Davis, of Acton, and a Mr. Hosmer. Our people then fired over one another's heads, being in a long column, two and two; they killed two and wounded eleven. Lieutenant Hawkstone, said to be the greatest beauty of the British army, had his cheeks so badly wounded that it disfigured him much, of which he bitterly complained. On this, the British fled, and assembled on the hill, the north side of Concord, and dressed their wounded, and then began their retreat. As they descended the hill near the road that comes out from Bedford they were pursued; Colonel Bridge, with a few men from Bedford and Chelmsford, came up, and killed several men. We pursued them and killed some; when they got to Lexington, they were so close pursued and fatigued, that they must have soon surrendered, had not Lord Percy met them with a large reinforcement and two field-pieces. They fired them, but the balls went high over our heads. But no cannon ever did more execution, such stories of their effects had been spread by the tories through our troops, that from this time more wont back than pursed. We pursued to Charlestown Common, and then retired to Cambridge."

****

This is part of a newspaper article printed in *The Massachusetts Spy*, May 3, 1775. The article was clearly written to foster anger toward the British.

"Americans! Forever bear in mind the BATTLE OF LEXINGTON where British Troops, unmolested and unprovoked wantonly, and in a most inhuman manner fired upon and killed a number of our countrymen, then robbed them of their provisions, ransacked, plundered and burnt their houses! Nor could the tears of defenseless women, some of whom were in the pains of childbirth, the cries of helpless, babes, nor the prayers of old age, confined to beds of sickness, appease their thirst for blood! – or divert them from the DESIGN of MURDER and ROBBERY!

CONCLUSION

"History is written by the victors."
—Winston Churchill

Did we gain our independence through acts of treason or through acts of patriotism? The simple solution is, that the winning side gets to choose the answer to that question. However, to be fair you cannot look at what happened on April 19, 1775 through the eyes of today's world. The event must be looked at through the eyes of the people in 1775.

Many Americans, particularly in the New England colonies, believed they were being pushed into a revolution by an oppressive government. They were Englishmen, yet they were not granted the rights and privileges that Englishmen in the mother country enjoyed.

They believed that liberty, a gift from God, was due all men, and if this gift was being denied then they had a right and an obligation to fight for it. They felt they were not asking for anything out of the ordinary, rather they were asking for what their countrymen back home in England enjoyed….liberty. Since they were willing to give up their lives for freedom and liberty they believed they were patriots.

Were there atrocities committed by the Americans? Not taking into the account of the young boy that killed the wounded British soldier with his ax the answer would be yes. These Americans, for the most part, were hard people that were capable of most anything. Many were former Indian fighters who asked for and showed no mercy. Hatred for the British had been building for years, plus there was even more hatred for the local Tories.

The militiamen also broke a gentlemen's rule of combat; you never target the officers. The officers were necessary to keep the common soldiers in check and make sure that the rules of combat were followed. The Americans found it was to their advantage to shoot the officers, or to cut the head off the snake.

The Americans looked upon the actions of the British as acts of terrorism. The Americans could have their property taken away without recourse. They could be taxed without any input from their leaders. If the Americans spoke out they could be jailed, beaten, or in some extreme cases killed for protesting the actions of the British government.

To the British the Americans were nothing more than bands of rebels committing treason, and they should not be considered patriots. They were not real soldiers and did not need to be treated as such. They were hiding weapons to use on the British soldiers who were there to protect the people and keep the peace. Besides, the rebels were in the minority, while the majority of the colonists supported British rule or they were indifferent to it.

Were there atrocities committed by the British? How could there not be? The British looked upon the colonists as second class citizens, and not true Englishmen, which would have justified the mistreatment of them. The common British soldier was in a strange land surrounded by people that showed him little respect. In fact, many colonists were better off that the soldiers and yet they were the ones complaining.

The British considered the militiamen savages, uncivilized, and very capable of committing unspeakable acts against the King's soldiers. After all, they fought behind walls, trees, and buildings, and after firing they would run away like cowards. Civilized soldiers faced each other out in the open and kept firing at each other until one side withdrew.

So were the rebels on April 19, 1775 a band of rebels committing treason, or a band of patriots? The answer depended on which side of the ocean you lived on. At the end of a war the victors write the history of the events and selects the names used to identify the winners.

****

"Our nation owes a debt to its fallen heroes that we cannot fully repay. But we can honor their sacrifice, and we must. We must honor it in our own lives by holding their memories close to our hearts, and heeding the example they set."

President Barack Obama
Arlington National Cemetery, 2011

INDEX

A

Abbott, Joseph, 60

Acton, 37,38,71,75,105,115

Adair, Lt. Jesse, 33

Adams, Deacon Joseph, 89

Adams, Samuel, 13-15,15,20,22-25,32,60

Andover, 39,40

Angle, Bloody, 52, 82

Apphia, 42

Aspinwall, Dr. William, 41, 97,98

B

Bacon, Lt. John, 50,103

Baker, Amos,74,76

Baldwin, Colonel Loammi, 84

Ballard, John, 12

Barber, Edward,98,104

Barker, Francis, 38

Barker, Lt. John, 30

Barrett, Amos, 66

Barrett, Colonel James, 67,70,71,77

Barrett, Meliscent, 30

Barrett, Stephen,68

Barrett, Deacon Thomas,72

Barron, Captain Oliver, 44

Batherick Mother, 84

Beaton, John, 79

Bedford, 16, 40,42,64,65,71,82,103,115

Belnap, James, 83

Belnap, Joe, 83

Benson, Able, 49

Bently, Joshua, 19

Beverly, 41,42,105

Bigelow, Captain Timothy, 54

Billerica, 40,42,80

Brookline, 41,91

Boston,11-15,18-20,22,25,26,29,30,34,37,40-50,53,54,56,79,83,89,96,100,103,108-110

Boston, Siege of, 101

Bowman, Samuel, 33

Bowman, Thaddeus, 34

Bridge, Brighton,78,83

Bridge, North, 38,47,48,53,68-70,73-79,94,107,115

Bridge, South, 68

Brookline, 97,104

Brooks, Rev. Edward, 48

Brooks, Joshua,76

Brown, John, 65,102

Brown, Reuben, 29,65,79

Brown, Solomon, 12,14,15,17,27,58

Buckman, John 58

Bunker Hill, Battle of, 37,46,52,100,103

Burdoo, Silas, 35

Burlington, 32

Buttrick, Major John, 65,74,75,77

C

Cambridge,19,22,23,28,31,33 40,42,45,50,51,78,79,83,86,89,97,99,102,103,112

Chamberlain, Nathaniel, 50,103

Charlestown, 19,20,23,31,53,98,100,101,104,108,109,112

Chelsea, 43

Chelmsford, 43,44,65,80,115

Child, Captain Lemuel, 52

Church, Old North, 19,24

Clarke, Rev. Jonas, 13,22,25,32,90

Clarke, Jonas Jr., 32,55-58,61,90

Conant, Colonel, 23

Cook, Israel, 48

Cook, Samuel, 44,104

Coolidge, Joseph,104

Cooper, Benjamin,94

Cooper, Rachel, 94

Corner, Merriam's, 40,42,44,53,79,81,82,103

Corner, Watson's, 42,46,97,102,104

Cummings, Samuel, 51

Cutter, Ammi, 74,83,92

Cutter, Deacon Ephraim, 88

D

Daland, Benjamin, 44,104

Danvers, 41,46,92,104

Davis, Captain Isaac, 38,74,75,105,115

Dawes, William, 18,19,22,24-27,52

Deavens, Richard, 20,23,24

De Bernice, Ensign, 46,69,70,84

Dedham, 44,45,104

Diamond, William, 35,64

Ditson, Thomas, 42

Douglass, Robert, 63,65

Downer, Eliphalet, 71

Draper, Captain William, 52

E

Eames, Captain James, 45

Eastabrook, Prince, 35,59

Eaton, Reuben, 52,81

Edgell, Captain Simon, 45,46

Edmunds, John, 48

Emerson, Ralph Waldo, 30

Emerson, Rev. William, 30,114

F

Farmingham, 46,80

Farrar, Samuel, 47

Faulkner, Colonel Francis, 37,38

Ferritt, Caesar, 85

Ferritt, John, 85

Frisk, Ebenezer, 39

Fitch, Lydia, 40

Fletcher, Joseph, 43

Flint, Captain Samuel, 44

Flint, William,105

Ford, Sergeant John, 43,81

Foster, Rev. Edmund, 80,84

Frost, Captain Ephraim, 82, 84

Framingham, 45

Frye, Colonel James, 39

G

Gage,GeneralThomas, 11,14,15,18,21,30,33,34,40,56,65,94,108

Gage, Margaret, 15

Gardner, Isaac, 4,97,104

Gardner, Colonel Thomas, 48

Goldthwait, Ebenezer, 44,104

Gould, Lt. Edward T., 48,63

Greene, General Nathanael,100

Groton, 46,50,51,63

Guild, Captain Aaron, 44

Guild, Captain Joseph, 45

H

Handley, Charles, 47,77

Handley, Samuel, 59,102

Hadley, Thomas,105

Hall, Captain Isaac, 48

Hancock, John, 13-15,20,22-25,32,34,35

Hancock, Lydia, 58,65

Harrington, Caleb, 22,59,102

Harrington, Jonathon,59,102

Hartwell, Mary, 28, 46,82

Hartwell, Samuel, 83

Hartwell, Sergeant Samuel, 16,28

Hastings, Samuel, 46

Haven, Elias, 104

Haynes, Deacon Josiah, 53,105

Hayward, James, 38,39

Hayward, Samuel, 39,85

Heath, General William, 89,90,100

Hemenway, Ebenezer, 46

Hicks, John, 42,97,102

Hill, Brook's, 45,81

Hill, Bullard's, 49

Hill, Fisk, 84,85

Hill, Pierce's, 89

Hill, Prospect, 97-99

Hill, Winter, 98

Hoar, Leonard, 82

Hosmer, Abner, 38,75,105,115

Howe, General William, 17

Hulton, Anne, 79,109,110

Hunt, Captain, 37

Hutchinson, Captain Israel, 41,44

I

Ishmael (slave, 99

J

Jacobs, Henry, 104

Jackson, Colonel Michael, 50,86

Johnston, Nicholas, 21

Jones, Elisha, 69

Jones, Ephraim, 71

K

Kendall, Deacon Obadiah, 63

Kennison, Reuben, 41,42,105

Kingsbury, Captain Caleb, 49

L

Lampson, David, 83,84

Laurie, Captain Walter, 69,71,74,75,107

Lee, Robert E., 102

Lincoln, 46,47,53,54,65,66,82,84

Littleton, 47

Locke, Captain Benjamin, 33 ,49

Longley, William, 52

Loring, Jonathan, 32,34,35

Lynn, 47,105

M

Malden, 48

Manning, Eliphalet, 53

Marcy, William, 42,97,102

Marrett, Rev.,32

Mead, Matthew, 14,83

Medford, 23,24,48,49,90,100,103

Menotomy,23,31,33,41,43,47,48,52,81,83,88,89,94,102-105

Merrimack, 39

Miller, James, 98,104

Mills, Amos, 50

Mills, Elisha, 50

Mitchell, Major Edward, 11,27,28,33

Monroe, Nathaniel, 40

Monroe, Timothy, 47,92,93

Moulton, Martha, 72,73

Mulliken, Lydia, 26

Munroe, Ebenezer, 57

Munroe, Jedediah, 57,102

Munroe, John, 57,58

Munroe, Robert, 59,102

Munroe, Sergeant William, 14,25,35

Muzzy, Isaac, 59,102

N

Needham, 44,49

Negroes, 45,99

Nelson, Josiah,16

Newman, Robert, 19,20

Newton, 50,86

Nixon, Captain, 53

O

P

Page, Captain Cyrus, 40

Page, Nathaniel, 40

Parker,CaptainJohn,26,29,33-36,56,60,62-65,79,84,102,11465,79,84,102

Parker, Jonas, 59,84

Parker, Jonathan, 50

Parker, Captain Moses, 44

Parkhurst, Samuel,43

Parsons, Captain Lawrence, 70,77-79

Payson, Rev. Samuel Phillips, 43,93

Pepperell, 50,51

Percy, General Hugh, 17,18,41,51,73,78,81,83-85,88-92,97,98,108-110,112

Perry, Elizabeth, 100

Pickering, Colonel Thomas, 52

Pierce, Benjamin, 52,104

Pitcairn,MajorJohn,20,21,33,34,55-58,60,68,71,84,85,88

Plympton, Thomas, 53

Pole, Captain Munday, 68

Polly, William, 49,103

Pond, Spy, 84

Porter, Asahel, 54, 59

Prescott, Abel, 46,77

Prescott, Dr. Samuel, 26-30, 46,53

Prescott, General, 50

Prince, Captain Asa, 44

Pulling, Captain John, 19,30

Putnam, Henry, 48,103

Putnam, Israel, 85

Putnam, Perely, 104

Q

Quincy, Dorothy, 32,58,65

R

Ramsdell, Abednego, 47,105

Rand, Elizabeth, 31

Raymond, John, 88,102

Reading, 42,52,88

Revere, Paul, 18,20,24-26,28,29,32,34-36,46,48,49

Richardson, Josiah, 59

Richardson, Moses, 42

Richardson, Thomas, 19

Road, Battle, 41,45,50,79,103,105

Robins, John, 62

Robinson, Lt. Colonel John, 74,115

Roxbury, 22,52,78,101,112

Russell House, 52,104,105

Russell, Jason, 41,49,91,92,103

Russell, Thomas, 83

S

Salem, 28,52,104

Sanderson, Elijah, 17,22,28,35,58,113,114

Shattuck, Sarah Hartwell, 51

Shirley, 52

Simonds, Joshua,98

Smith, Captain William, 28, 46

Smith,ColonelFrancis,11,17,20-22,30,31,33,34,41,56,58,6567-68,71,73-75,77-79,81,84,87,88,89,92,101,106,107,108,112

Somerset, 20,100

Somerville, 99,100

Southwick, George, 44,104

Spaulding, Lt. Colonel Simeon, 43

Stevens, James, 40

Stow, 52,80

Sudbury, 46,53,80,81,103

Sutherland, Lt., 33,56,75

T

Tavern, Black Horse, 33

Tavern, Buckman's, 15,17,26,29,32,34,58,60,64,84

Tavern, Bullard's, 49

Tavern, Cooper's, 83,94,96

Tavern, Fitch's, 40,42

Tavern, Kettell's, 48

Tavern, Munroe's, 14,88

Tavern, Newell's, 32

Tavern, Widow Brown's, 77,78

Tavern, Wright's, 30,71,72

Tewksbury, 40,53

Thatcher, Captain Sam, 42

Thaxter, Rev. Joseph, 86,114,115

Thompson, Abijah, 54

Thompson, Daniel, 47,103

Thorning, William, 82

Tidd, Benjamin, 60

Tidd, John, 58

Tories, 16,51,116

Townsend, Daniel, 47,92,93,105

Tredwell, Rev. 43

Trull, Captain John, 53

Tufts, Dr. Cotton, 96

Tufts, John,100

Tufts, Samuel, 31

U

Underwood, Joseph, 60

V

W

War, French and Indian, 33, 44,67,81,83

Warren, Dr. Joseph, 11,12,15,18,19,25,89,90,100

Washington, George, 25,101

Watertown, 90,104

Webb, Jotham, 92

Wellington, Benjamin, 34

Westford, 53,74,80,115

White, Ammi, 78

"White Cockade", 38,53,74

White, Captain Thomas, 41

Whiting, Captain Moses, 51,52

Whittemore, Samuel, 32,33,91

Willard, Thomas Rice, 61

Wilson, Captain Jonathan, 41,82,103

Winship, Jason, 49,94

Winship, Simon, 62

Woburn, 53,54,63,65,80,82,90,103

Wood, Sylvanus, 63,65

Woodbury, James, 38

Woods, Amos, 73

Worcester, 54

Wright, David, 51

Wright, Prudence, 51

Wyman, Jabez, 49,94,103

Wyman, Nathaniel, 102

X

Y

Yankee Doodle, 74,78

Z

Bibliography

Abbatt, William, editor, *Memoirs of Major-General William Heath by Himself.* New York, New York: William Abbatt, 1901.

Adams, John, *Letter to Lemuel Shattuck, Esq, of Boston from Josiah Adams, Esq. of Framingham, in Vindication of the Claims of Captain Isaac Davis of Acton to His Just Share in the Honors of the Concord Fight also Depositions of Witnesses, Stating the Facts on Which the Claims are Founded.* Boston, Massachusetts: Damrell & Moore, 1850.

Adams, Josiah, *An Address Delivered at Acton, July 21, 1835 of the Organization of that Town.* Boston, Massachusetts: J.T. Buckingham, 1835.

Anonymous, *The Shot Heard Around the World From Lexington to Yorktown, A Pictorial History of the American Revolution.* Boston, Massachusetts: John Adams Lee Publishing Company, 1892.

Bailey, Sarah Loring, *Historical Sketches Andover Massachusetts.* Boston, Massachusetts: Houghton, Mifflin & Co., 1880.

Bolton, Charles Knowles, editor, *Letters of Hugh Earl Percy from Boston and New York 1774-1776.* Boston, Massachusetts: Charles E. Goodspeed, 1902.

_____, *A Bridge to the Past.* A Teacher's guide to the North Bridge and Battle Road Units of Minute Man National Historical Park, 2000.

Brooks, Charles, *History of the Town of Medford, Middlesex County, Massachusetts.* Boston, Massachusetts: James M. Usher, 1855.

Brown, Abram English, *Beneath Old Roof Trees.* Boston, Massachusetts: Lee and Shepard, 1896.

Brown, Abram English, *Town of Bedford, Middlesex County, Massachusetts, From Its Earliest Settlement to the Year of Our Lord, 1891.* Bedford, Massachusetts: Published by Author, 1891.

Butler, Caleb, *History of the Town of Groton Including Pepperell and Shirley,* Boston, Massachusetts: Press of T.R. Marvin, 1848.

Chamberlain, Mellen, *A Documentary History of Chelsea Vol. 1.* Boston, Massachusetts: Massachusetts Historical Society, 1908.

Chandler, Seth, *History of the Town of Shirley Massachusetts.* Shirley, Massachusetts: Published by the Author, 1883.

Chase, Ellen, *The Beginnings of the American Revolution: Based on Contemporary Letters Diaries and Other Document.* New York, New York: Baker and Taylor, 1910.

Clarke, George Kuhn, *History of Needham, Massachusetts 1711-1911.* Needham, Massachusetts: University Press, 1911.

Coburn, Frank Warren, *The Battle of April 19, 1775, in Lexington, Concord, Lincoln, Arlington, Cambridge, Somerville, and Charlestown, Massachusetts.* Lexington, Massachusetts: Published by the Author, 1912.

Coburn, Silas R., *History of Dracut Massachusetts.* Lowell, Massachusetts: Press of the Courier-Citizen Co., 1922.

Corey, Deloraine Pendre, *The History of Malden Massachusetts 1633-1785.* Malden, Massachusetts: Published by the Author, 1899.

Crowder, Jack Darrell, *Chaplains of the Revolutionary War: Black Robed American Warriors,* Jefferson, North Carolina: McFarland, 2017.

Cutter, Benjamin, and William R. Cutter, *History of the Town of Arlington Massachusetts or District of Menotomy.* Boston, Massachusetts: David Clapp & Son, 1880.

Cutter, William Richard, *Genealogical and Personal Memoirs Relating to the Families of the State of Massachusetts, Vol. 1.* New York, New York: Lewis Historical Publishing Co., 1910.

Dobbs, John F., *From Bunker Hill to Manila Bay A Record of Battles.* New York, New York: Published by Author, 1906.

Eaton, Lilley, *Genealogical History of the Town of Reading, Mass. Including the Present Towns of Wakefield, Reading, and North Reading.* Boston, Massachusetts: Alfred Mudge & Son, 1874.

French, Allen, *The Day of Concord and Lexington, the Nineteenth of April, 1775.* Boston, Massachusetts: Little, Brown, and Company, 1925.

Frothingham, Richard, *The History of Charlestown Massachusetts.* Boston Massachusetts: Charles C. Little and James Brown, 1845.

Frothingham, Richard, *History of the Siege of Boston and of the Battles of Lexington and Concord and Bunker Hill.* Boston, Massachusetts: Little, Brown, and Company, 1873.

Gettemy, Charles Ferris, *The True Story of Paul Revere: His Midnight Ride and Court-Martial, His Useful Public Services.* Boston, Massachusetts: Little, Brown, and Company, 1905.

Hafner, Donald, *First Blood Shed in the Revolution: The Tale of Josiah Nelson on April 19, 1775.* Boston College University Libraries, 2015.

Hallahan, William H., *The Day the American Revolution Began.* New York, New York: Perennial, 2000.

Hazen, Rev. Henry A., *History of Billerica, Massachusetts,* Boston, Massachusetts: A. William & Co., 1883.

_____, *Historical Structure Report on Hancock-Clarke House*, Lexington Historical Society.

Hodgman, Rev. Edwin R., *History of the Town of Westford in the County of Middlesex, Massachusetts 1659-1833.* Lowell, Massachusetts: Morning Mail Company, 1883.

Hudson, Alfred Sereno, *The History of Sudbury, Massachusetts.* Sudbury, Massachusetts: Published by the Town of Sudbury, 1889.

Hudson, Charles, *History of the Town of Lexington Middlesex County, Massachusetts Vol. 1.* Boston, Massachusetts: Houghton Mifflin, 1912.

Hurd, Hamilton, *History of Middlesex County, Massachusetts with Biographical Sketches, Vol. III.* Philadelphia, Pennsylvania: J.W. Lewis & Co., 1890.

Hurd, Hamilton, *History of Norfolk County, Massachusetts with Biographical Sketches.* Philadelphia, Pennsylvania: J.W. Lewis & Company, 1884.

Johnston, Henry, P., editor, *Record of Connecticut Men in the Military and Naval Service During the War of the Revolution 1775-1783.* Hartford, Connecticut: Hartford, 1889.

Lewis, Alonso, and James Newhall, *History of Lynn 1629-1864.* Lynn, Massachusetts: George C. Herbert, 1890.

Lincoln, William, *History of Worcester, Massachusetts.* Worcester, Massachusetts: Charles Hersey, 1862.

Lincoln, William, *The Journals of the Provincial Congress of Massachusetts in 1774 and 1775 and of the Committee of Safety.* Boston, Massachusetts: Dutton and Wentworth, 1837.

Lossing, Benson, J., *The Pictorial Field-Book of the Revolution Vol. I.* New York, New York: Harper Brothers, 1860.

Ludlum, David, *"The Weather of Independence". In The County Journal New England Weather Book.* Boston, Massachusetts, 1976.

Lewis, Alonso and James R. Newhall, *History of Lynn.* Lynn, Massachusetts: George C. Herbert, 1890.

MacKenzie, Frederick, *Description of the Battle of Lexington by Lieutenant MacKenzie of the Royal Welsh Fusileers.* Cambridge, Massachusetts: Harvard University Press, 1926.

Malcolm, Joyce Lee, *Peter's War, A New England Slave Boy and the American Revolution.* New Haven, Connecticut: Yale University Press, 2008.

Moore, Frank, *Diary of the American Revolution from Newspapers and Original Documents, Vol I.* New York, New York: Charles Scribner, 1859.

Muzzey, A.B., *Reminiscences and Memorials of Men of the Revolution and Their Families.* Boston, Massachusetts: Estes and Lauriat, 1883.

Newspaper, *The Massachusetts Spy,* Worchester, Massachusetts, May 5, 1775.

Paige, Lucius R., *History of Cambridge Massachusetts 1630-1877.* Boston, Massachusetts: H.O. Houghton and Company, 1877.

Parr, James L., Kevin A. Swope, *Framingham Legends and Lore.* South Carolina: History Press, 2009.

Polland, Henry, W., *William Dawes and His Ride with Paul Revere.* Boston, Massachusetts: John Wilson & Son, 1878.

Pride, Edward D., *Tewksbury--A Short History.* Cambridge, Massachusetts: Tewksbury Improvement Association, 1888.

Ripley, Rev. Ezra, *A History of the Fight at Concord on the 19th of April, 1775.* Concord, Massachusetts: Herman Atwill, 1832.

Sewall, Samuel, *The History of Woburn, Massachusetts*. Boston, Massachusetts: Wiggin and Lunt, 1868.

Smith, Samuel Abbot, *West Cambridge on the 19th of April, 1775, an Address Delivered in Behalf of the Ladies Soldiers Aid Society of West Cambridge*. Boston, Massachusetts: Alfred Mudge & Sons, 1864.

Smith, S.F., *History of Newton Massachusetts Town and City*. Boston, Massachusetts: The American Logotype Co., 1880.

Stone, Edwin, M., *History of Beverly*. Boston, Massachusetts: James Munroe and Company, 1843.

Tapley, Harriet Silvester, *Chronicles of Danvers Old Salem Village Massachusetts 1632-1923*. Danvers, Massachusetts: Danvers Historical Society, 1923.

Temple, J.H., *History of Framingham, Massachusetts 1640-1880*. Framingham, Massachusetts: Published by the Town, 1887.

Tourtellot, Author, *William Diamond's Drum, The Beginning of the War of the American Revolution*. New York, New York: Doubleday & Company, 1949.

The United States Literary Gazette, Vol. 1 from April 1824 to April, 1825. Boston, Massachusetts: Cummings, Hillard, & Son, 1825.

Waters, Rev. Wilson, *History of Chelmsford Massachusetts*. Lowell, Massachusetts: Courier-Citizen Co., 1917.

Wellman, Thomas, *History of the Town of Lynnfield, Massachusetts*. Lynnfield, Massachusetts: Blanchard & Watts, 1885.

Wild, Helen Tilden, *Medford in the Revolution. Military History of Medford, Massachusetts 1765-1783*. Medford, Massachusetts: J.C. Miller, Jr., 1908.

Woodbury, Ellen C.D.Q., *Dorothy Quincy Wife of John Hancock with Events of her Time*. Washington and New York: The Neale Publishing Co., 1905.

Woods, Harriet R., *Historical Sketches of Brookline, Massachusetts*. Boston, Massachusetts: Robert S. Davis and Company, 1874.

Worthington, Erastus, *The History of Dedham*. Boston, Massachusetts: Dutton & Wentworth, 1827.

Government Records

Census records. Ancestry.com database.

Connecticut Town Birth Records. Ancestry.com database.

Massachusetts Soldiers & Sailors in the War of Revolution. Ancestry.com database.

Massachusetts Town & Vital Records 1620-1988. Ancestry.com database.

New Hampshire, Death & Burial Records 1654-1949. Ancestry.com database.

Non Mohawk Valley Pensioners N-Z. Ancestry.com database.

Pension List of 1792-1795. Ancestry.com database.

Service of Connecticut Men in the War of the Revolution. Ancestry.com database.

U.S. Pension Records. Ancestry.com database.

U.S. Pensioners 1818-1872. Ancestry.com database.

U.S. Revolutionary War Rolls 1775-1783. Ancestry.com database.

www.ingramcontent.com/pod-product-compliance
Lightning Source LLC
Chambersburg PA
CBHW080437230426
43662CB00015B/2302